I0817469

Virgin

## ALSO BY HOLLIE MCNISH

Lobster
Slug
Antigone
Plum
Nobody Told Me
Offside *(with Sabrina Mahfouz)*
Cherry Pie
Papers

### AUDIO

Versus
Hollie and the Metropole Orkest

# Hollie McNish

# Virgin

FLEET

FLEET

First published in Great Britain in 2025 by Fleet

1 3 5 7 9 10 8 6 4 2



A CIP catalogue record for this book
is available from the British Library.

ISBN 978-0-349-12744-6

Typeset in Garamond by M Rules
Printed and bound in Great Britain by
Clays Ltd, Elcograf S.p.A.

Papers used by Fleet are from well-managed forests
and other responsible sources.

Fleet
An imprint of
Little, Brown Book Group
Carmelite House
50 Victoria Embankment
London EC4Y 0DZ

The authorised representative
in the EEA is
Hachette Ireland
8 Castlecourt Centre
Dublin 15, D15 XTP3, Ireland
(email: info@hbgi.ie)

An Hachette UK Company
www.hachette.co.uk

www.littlebrown.co.uk

To all those people I knew and didn't know

blamed, shamed, pressured, tortured
de-humanised, de-mothered

over a man-made concept
about your own body

i'm so sorry
for your
loss

.

i hope
you enjoy
these poems

i hope you enjoy
your body, and i hope

no one is able to convince us
for any longer that we are less pure,

less whole, because of an idea created by
those in power to control our minds and flesh

*for my daughter,*
*who made sure i didn't*
*miss the snow*

**it doesn't snow much here,**

so every time the silent sky dresses all the world with white
i am five years old again, gloves and scarf already on
noses pressed against the sweat-frost of the window pane
praying this soft blossom will settle on the surface
make the world a canvas for our imaginations once again

overnight it came this time, we woke to streets a glowing white
fled doors with hurried slams to paint the winter's page in footprint pens
and as we ran, we scoured the snow for all the markings made before;
first paw prints of a fox and cub, a robin's hops, quicker children's outlines
fallen to embrace the snow with outstretched arms in angel moulds

until the snow falls heavy once again
or else melts in sun and showers
reawakening the colours

## Chapter Two
Making Shame: Hell is Where the Hemline is



## Chapter Three
Making Memories: Life, Pre-loved

## Chapter Four
Making Laws: Wolves and Warnings

**Chapter Five**
Making Love

# INTRODUCTION

Life is full of first times: first breath, first scream, first hug, first tears, first sip of milk. First steps. First word. First fib. First fight. First friends, first fallouts. A first kiss. A first cry for help. A first *I love you*. First break up. The first time you feel a vivid dream disappear with morning yawns. A first nightmare. Your first taste of a ripe mango. The first time you ride a bike without stabilisers, screaming *don't let go* before realising you're already there. The first book you take out of a library with your own library card. Your first paddle in ocean. First wobbly tooth, half-hanging from your gums, all sharp-jelly fascination. Your first pay cheque. The first time you see a stranger cry. A first orgasm, by yourself, with another. The first time someone you love dies.

So many firsts. Some delicious, divine. Some formative. Some springboards to better second and thirds and more. Some uninspiring, forgotten. Some desperately traumatic. But not one of them sold to us with such cultural heavy lifting as the first time a penis moves in and out of a vagina. No, of all the first times I have had and am yet to have in this peek at being human, of all the human life experiences we may undergo throughout the years we are alive on this living, spinning planet, not one single other moment has been sold as being powerful enough to apparently change our entire state of being – from virgin to non-virgin – as this. The more I think about it, the more ridiculous, and dangerous, it becomes.

*Have you lost your virginity yet?* was a recurring conversation throughout my teens. From the age of about twelve to twenty, we spoke about who was a virgin, who wasn't, who might be, who might not be soon, who pretended they weren't but were, and vice versa. We argued about what counted, definitely, probably, possibly. We watched horror films in which losing your virgin status as a young woman made you more prone to being murdered, comedies about forty-year-old virgin men, and we laughed, and we panicked.

Whatever our personal pressures, concerns or commitments were towards our so-called virginity, we talked about it, and were taught about it, as if it were some sort of concrete fact of the flesh.

Please note: in this book, when I write the word sex, I mean all and any forms of sex. I'm sick of 'sex' being sold as intercourse only, when it's so much more. If I mean intercourse specifically, I'll say that.

Most importantly, when I refer to sexual experiences, I mean consensual activity. There is no such thing as non-consensual sexual activity. The word for that is rape or abuse and those are the only words I will use for those things now, in both my writing and my life.

I love touch. I love kissing, snogging, stroking, sex and so on. I find touch such a positive idea and I am determined not to let anyone who has abused or bullied mine or anyone else's body have all those words related to touch for themselves.

I've had lips on my lips I didn't want on my lips. I'm not calling that a kiss any more. I love the word kiss too much, all snake-swift and kettle clicks. No, that was no kiss, it was abuse. I've had a tongue forced into my mouth and across my cheeks and neck that I tried desperately to remove and couldn't. That old creep didn't lick or snog me. No, I like licks and snogs. I like the music of those simple little words, onomatopoeic masterpieces. That was abuse. I've had hands grapple through my car window uninvited onto my breasts. I'm not describing that as touching, or stroking, or even groping. I like touching and stroking and enamoured groping too much. That was abuse. One of the first times I had fingers inside me, I said *get off*, and was ignored. I'm not describing that as my first time getting fingered. I like the word fingered too much; it's a ridiculous and giggly word, so damn practical, so damn good if deftly carried out. No, that finger in me, that was abuse. My first time getting fingered was excellent. I mean, it was terrible and awkward as fuck, but it was excellent.

Of course, it's not always that simple, and it is an arduous and at times harrowing process to shift my mindset, but words have power and if it wasn't consensual, you're not having it any more. You've had enough of me already.

You're not having my first times. Or second times. None of them. And you're not having the poetry.

My first attempt at intercourse was nice. It did not hurt, as rightly it should not, no matter the horrendous narrative about first time pain being some sort of marker of purity. I lost nothing except a sandal. The second time was better. The fifth time was my favourite with him. I have since had much nicer sexual experiences than any of that first year, mainly due to knowing my own body better, being less ashamed of pleasure, and actually talking to the human being I am with.

I think this is how most consensual experience works. After practising, and reading more recipes, and becoming more confident, I am now much better at making lasagne than my first few soggy attempts.

The morning after that first time, despite no longer believing in the concept of virginity, I still found myself standing in front of his bathroom mirror searching some sort of solid change – loss – in my appearance; slightly convinced that my friends and family would somehow see the great change in me. It is so difficult to shake beliefs which have been drummed into you since childhood.

Virginity wasn't a new idea to me that arrived overnight with puberty. It was embedded into my brain from very early on. By the age of five, I had heard the word virgin numerous times; us girls excited to see who would be picked to play the star lead capital-lettered Virgin in the primary school nativity play. I knew, before any other sexual education, before any discussion of touch or consent, that it was virginity which made Mary – this *mother* – better, special, impossible to mimic. Joseph's virginity was never mentioned. We didn't call him Virgin Joseph. Of course we fucking didn't.

I'm now a fully grown adult, and all around me, the world still reels from the effects of this ephemeral concept; from the continued pressure to lose or not lose this label, to the shame, ostracisation and atrocities that stem from a view of what is pure and what is not; based almost entirely upon the belief in this man-made virgin myth.

For years, I've had this concept in the back of my mind because I am utterly fascinated, terrified and bewildered by the way in which it still causes so much worry, wonder, war. These poems are all the wavering and wanderings my mind has done thinking about the power of this soft, six-letter word.

I began thinking about who gains from this pervasive shame. Who gets a thrill from it. What atrocities are we being distracted from as we obsess over how much sexual experience somebody may or may not have had. I began imagining a virginless world. No, not a world where there are no people who've not had intercourse, just a world where that concept is gone and we are allowed to choose for ourselves what our most transformative experiences have been. I began thinking of all the other related obsessions we have with newness and first times and untouched and single-use and throwaway and damaged. I started to think of my grandparents' house, which had two living rooms, one of which we were rarely allowed to go in; a room saved perfectly neat and new in case the vicar came to visit, their wedding china still on display in the cupboard, saved untouched for special occasions that never came; and how I now use this crockery every day for my dinner. I wonder whether they'd be pleased, relieved or raging at me for that.

I so often think what love could be, growing up: mind, bodies, pleasure, sex, all of it, how gorgeous, if it was all anchored around consent, and joy. Leave the kids the fuck alone to go on the swings. Give teenagers the knowledge they need, and leave them to love amongst themselves; you have no right to the vulnerabilities of their youth. Stop shaming fully consenting adults for loving in ways someone at some point has deemed unsuitable. Help victims of abuse without blaming and shaming. Help more people feel comfortable seeking help. And stop castigating yourself over an invented concept.

Once you're done with this book, feel free to pass it on to someone else. Feel free to scribble in it, underline bits you like or don't; decorate it with your thoughts. Write a poem on an empty page or in the margins. That's where most of my poems begin. In other people's books. Feel free to make the paper pages ripple because you've read it in the bath and accidentally dropped it in the water. Dry it in the sun.

If it's borrowed from the library, ignore the above, but thank you. I love libraries and I love you for supporting them.

However you read it, I hope you enjoy some of the poems. Mainly, they are love poems.

# CHAPTER ONE

## *Making Myths: From Apple Trees to Jump Humping*

*A penis is not powerful enough*
*to change a woman's worth*
*via simple insertion*

– DR LAURIE MINTZ

*Myths which are believed in tend to become true*

– attributed to GEORGE ORWELL

we are not. we are not. we are not. we are not. we are not. we are not. we are not.
we are not. we are not. we are not. we are not. we are not. we are not. we are not.
we are not. we are not. we are not. we are not. we are not. we are not. we are not.

some apples
fell much too soon
bruised upon the ground
for the squirrels or soil to scoff;
others dangled brazenly above, until
tiptoe-plucked from ever-heaving branches,
eaten at their sweetest; many appeared undamaged
only to discover holes, softened, powdered, browning
inside tunnels burrowed from bugs that came before –
bitten, then regretted; others grabbed and gobbled up
by ravenous passing strangers bereft of self-control;
and now, apple season almost over, just a handful,
steadfast to their stalks, determined not to drop;
oh untouched fruits of autumn, clinging on
as all the others, picked or fallen,
succumb to winter's rot.
there is no
metaphor
here;
those
are
apples

we are not. we are not. we are not. we are not. we are not. we are not. we are not.
we are not. we are not. we are not. we are not. we are not. we are not. we are not.
we are not. we are not. we are not. we are not. we are not. we are not. we are not.

## swimming

when i say sex, i mean sex. consensual and true. otherwise i'd say rape. otherwise i'd say abuse. when i say kiss, i mean kiss. i mean lip lips, i mean cheek neck, i mean yes and peck and snog and please and mouth and leaf and blossom. otherwise i'd say abuse. otherwise i'd say coercion. when i say eating, i don't mean choking. when i say swimming, i don't mean drowning. i mean swimming. i mean swimming. i mean swimming. i mean swimming. i mean swimming.

## eating mashed potato with my parents after 'losing my virginity'

how do you stand like a non-virgin? i wondered
feet shuffling the door mat to my parents' house
my index finger helicoptering the doorbell like an unlicensed landing pad
fuck, how did i ring it last month, last month
when my hands were still virgin hands?
just knock, hollie, they probably know already anyway,
can smell the scent of you, all sexual now, seeping through the letterbox,
*your face looks different?* your mum will say
*have you done something to your hair?*
fuck! put it in a ponytail!   my mother is a nurse after all
has seen every sort of body, virgins, non-virgins . . .   that's it i guess;
how did i used to stand when my feet were still virgin-toed?
hand off the hip, do you want the whole neighbourhood to know?
fuck, i bet there will be gravy, how will i pour the gravy
across the buttered mashed potato   i love buttered mashed potatoes
how did i eat it before? what if i start making non-virgin sex noises?
what if, fork to my now non-virgin lips
i slip the buttered mashed potato too sensually from the silver spoon,
and swallow, the mash, and say *mmm*, like *mmm,*
*that buttered mashed potato is so delicious*,
what if i pronounce the *o* in *so* too hard or too long, like *ooooh yeah*
like *soooo delicious*, like *mmm that's sooo delicious*,
and my parents look at me all weird across the table
and my hair does look different
what if i take a really big dollop, too big and too greedy
and a little of the buttered mashed potato drops onto my chin
like some sort of globulite of leftover sex cum
what if i need more water and i go to grab the handle of the jug
and my mum looks up, peas fidgeting suspiciously on her fork,
and says *i'll bet you do, hollie, i'll bet you're really, really thirsty*

**horror**

in the scary stories, sluts died first,
lay bleeding, screaming, in agony –
only virgins died beautifully

silent and sad, like paintings of unfed angels
in bathtubs, naked, pale, face up on a white god's
cold, hard floor; and we could cry then, cry

for the virgins. zoomed in, tiny rivulet of red
trickling neat from the corner of a rosebud mouth
onto newly settled snow; one clean, fetished bullet hole

unlike the sluts, make-up smudged, messy murders,
protective cloaks of chastity no longer soundproofing
their slaggish roars – beaten ugly, hair sweaty

only a virgin could approach the unicorn
only a virgin could break the spell
only a virgin's tears could heal him

in the scripts, virginity protected us
or at least made us more beautiful in death;
in life, it makes no difference

like carrying a gun for self-defence
more likely used against you

## your dead grandparents are not watching you wank

*for friends who have been told that their dearly departed loved ones are 'with you always'*

no need to hide under the covers, my friend, they are gone

relieved of their pain and the cumbersome clatter of bone
arthritic fingers and incurable cancers now life-dust for soil
their burden of body reborn into winds
your dead grandparents can swim between suns now
suffering gone, ghost-light and undone
unearthed and eternal, dissolved in the music of night
they are swallowing stars at the edge of the cosmos
drunk in the roots of the moons, the universe laid out
like forest   like meadow   like sea
floating      forever                              wherever they please,
and you worry, as they unleash the secrets of time,
every possible story now open to write
that most likely, *most* likely
they'll have rushed to your bedside,
desperate to peek at your haphazard strokes
as saliva incontinent drips from the wag of your tongue
and you cum, uuurgh, into clenched, sweaty hands, clammy-faced

    they are not, they *really* are not –

so wank away, my friend, wank away

**ditto god**

*for friends who have been told that their own hands touching their own body*
*will anger an almighty, who is watching them, always*

it just seems    slightly specific
for an almighty creator to bother about

after moulding in mastermind detail
a universe baubled by planets and suns

composing a world
from nothing and love

the bones of each whale born of star dust
and milk, forged from the blood of each mother

one ant, then another

just, a bit    out of character?
for an almighty to pay such close attention,
snooping in bedrooms

after birthing the soils and the oceans
perfecting the shape and the shade
of each leaf and each petal
to dance just so with the rainfall and sun
that each exact insect or zephyr or bird
may deliver their seeds into bloom

after painting with such holy detail
the tail of each peacock and lemur and comet

gifting each skylark its own golden notes

and our own cello-bodies –
skin surface glittered with nerves
like the night stuffed sky-full of stars
– so carefully crafted for song

**questions we asked when we were 'virgins'/**
**answers we were never given**

1. *if i touch myself, am i still a virgin?*

answer:
*virginity is a concept made up long ago*
*in times that also spoke positively of slavery and stoning*
*'give your daughters to us, and take our daughters for yourselves'*

2. *if i use a tampon, am i still a virgin?*

answer:
*virginity is a concept made up long ago*
*in times that also spoke positively of slavery and stoning*
*and selling your children to the neighbours in exchange for a goat*
*'give your daughters to us, and take our daughters for yourselves'*
*all it means is that you have not yet had sexual intercourse*
*do whatever helps the bleeding  be careful of the chemicals*
*last time i checked, tampons are not made of penis, also vice versa,*
*penises cannot be used as tampons, especially when swimming*

3. *if i bike ride and my hymen breaks, am i still a virgin?*
4. *if i put my finger in a little bit?*
5. *if i fantasise and use vibrators, only outside, but i orgasm?*
6. *if it was the tip of his penis but only for a second?*
7. *if his penis was near the entrance of my vagina*
*but we didn't move and someone else shook the bed?*
*(yes, this is a thing, look it up, the world is a dunce cap)*

answer:
*virginity is a concept is a concept is a concept*
*hymens are all different, all different, all different*

*if you want to, go ahead, have statuesque intercourse*
*enabled by someone else jumping on the bed beside you both*
*so that your genitals, through the force of the friend's jumping*
*rather than the chosen movement of your own bodies,*
*go into one another in what is very much the same action*
*as intercourse but you can still tell the pastor or the priest*
*or your father or your god or whoever else might be judging you*
*that you're still officially a virgin because, well, it was like*
*accidental falling, the force of the movement of the mattress*
*to blame for the penetration, fuck, it's your life,*
*if god is that specific, fair play to you,*
*it just seems a lot of effort for an ephemeral concept,*
*do what you want, personally, i prefer to separate sex and trampolining*

8. *if i only have anal sex, am i still a virgin?*

answer:
*fuck* [stops laughing, drops dramatically to the floor,
terrified, wondering how loudly the word
*concept concept concept* can be screamed
before the rise in teenage girls suffering from
anal ruptures from anal penetration
undertaken to avoid 'unholying' themselves
whilst still 'pleasing' a forceful fuckwit partner,
lowers] *i am so sorry this has happened*
*i am so sorry you are even considering this question*
*what stories are we still telling to our children?*
*virginity is a concept, hymens are all different,*
*the entrance to hell is not through your vagina,*
*don't do anything you do not want to,*
*anal sex is anal sex, coercion is coercion*

9. *if i am no longer a virgin am i broken?*
10. *if i am no longer a virgin am i damaged?*
11. *am i bad?*

answer:
*is a concept is a concept*
*is a concept is a concept*

12. *if i am abused, am i still a virgin?*
13. *if i am raped?*

[pause][breathe][sob][detonate]

[claws at own stomach, praying for scales
and scorched dragon breath that i may time-travel back
to the beginnings of this concept, burn to ash
the word 'virgin' before it is invented, or else gather up
all of the children on earth, stuff them back
inside the water of my womb
until we tell them the truth about their bodies]

*fuck virginity. fuck purity. fuck confession.*
*fuck holy. fuck hymns. fuck heaven. fuck hymen.*

14. our children, who art on earth

you are not a fruit tree plucked
nor a rose de-petalled
nor a box unlocked
nor a vase now shattered
nor a package now damaged
nor a patch of snow pissed on
nor an angel now fallen

nor any other metaphor dreamt up by shite poets . . .

virginity is a concept
virginity is power play
virginity is a sales pitch
virginity is a fetish
virginity is a brothel price
virginity is mistranslation
virginity is a crusade
virginity is a word
virginity is a porno
virginity is a dowry
virginity is a hoax
virginity is an honour kill
virginity is magdalene laundries
virginity is an asylum full of terrified teenage mothers
virginity is a paedophile
virginity is legislation to help grown men marry children
virginity is profit
virginity is a hymen reconstruction surgery receipt
virginity is possession
virginity is rape, just in case, before a taliban execution

questions asked by human beings on internet search engines this year

15. *how do i tell if my daughter is still a virgin*
16. *how do i check if my fiancée is a virgin*
17. *how could i check if i am still a virgin?*
18. *can a doctor check if my daughter is still a virgin?*
19. *what is virginity testing?*
20. *what is the two-finger hymen test?*
21. *how to accept a girl who is not a virgin?*
22. *can virginity be restored through surgery?*

23. *how painful is hymenoplasty?*
24. *can you regain your virginity after having sex?*
25. *can i still go to heaven if i am not a virgin?*

answer:
a twelve-year-old girl was tortured and murdered by her older brother when he saw her menstruation blood and assumed, because he knew nothing about menstruation, that she'd 'lost her virginity', thus deeming her impure, thus deeming it appropriate to kill her.

**jesus seemed cool though,**

spoke of love a lot – your neighbour,
yourself, the local women selling sex work.
everyone really, except the shareholders.

didn't seem the type to be bothered
by loving touch under the covers,
or to punish with hell-fire
two people making love.

*love everyone*, he said.
*love everyone*, he said again.
*love everyone*, he repeated.

seems like he meant it –
went to quite a lot of trouble
to prove his point.

**it's your anus, live your life**

i don't care if i die without doing anal
some dicks are so wide and i've no taste for pain
an oversized poo once injured my arsehole
the poor ruptured skin took so long to heal
and the graze kept reopening again and again

some of my best friends are anal enthusiasts –
sex toys lined up like russian doll butt plugs
*oh you must!* they declare, like passing round chocolates
rub lube on my hand like a perfume assistant
*start small, slowly make your way up . . .*

and it's kind that they care, but the weeks it would take
to gently ease the muscles apart
till they comfortably welcome his penis
just seems like a whole lot of effort
and there's still so much cheese left to eat in the fridge

so no, i don't care if i die without trying anal
i do care if i die without visiting cuba
a nipple orgasm, sleeper train romance,
an orgy perhaps, though they seem over-rated,
my friend went to one, hoping ballgowns and nibbles –
it was in someone's garage and mainly just men

and no, i won't *do it for him*          it's my anus,
not sweets you feel pressured to buy
to avoid a child's tantrum at checkout;
and no, i don't pressure him either
to push unwanted things up his arse

it's my anus, it functions, it's lovely
it's your anus, it's equally fine
so for now, i'll enjoy my chocolate eclair
and you, whatever feels right

**things which might hurt you**

injections, and tea sipped still piping hot,
hogweed trod in ankle socks, laughter
at a love note, low ceilings that you dodge
too late, but   intercourse should not . . .

not the first time, not the final time,
nor any in between. blood on sheets
was sought to shame.   pain
is not a metaphor for anything but pain

bathing naked in a lobster cage, baseball
with no baseball bat   friendlessness
a boxing match   being batman with no bat mask
picking blackberries with a blindfold on
gun laws   guns
drinking bleach (unless you're trump)

masturbating after making lunch, the remnants of hot, red chillies
forgotten on your fingertips – a burning rush for yoghurt
in an empty fridge, shower cold and focused on your clitoris or cock

yes, many things might hurt you
in life, so many things might hurt you, but
intercourse should not

## exchange rate

you gave us sun    we made pot noodles –
you gave us raindrops
seeds, breeze    a light, convenient snack
and pollinating insects    ready in two minutes

you gave us    we made sweets, shaped like
watermelons, cherries,    watermelons, cherries,
plums, pears and pomegranates    plums, pears and pomegranates

you gave us coral    we made trawler nets
you gave us fossils    we made plastic bags
you gave us wheat    we made lucky charms
you gave us faces    we made botox
you gave us heads, shoulders,    we made sin, virginity,
knees and toes, fingers,    silicone, profits,
clitorises and penises    insecurities and shame

you gave us clouds    we made acid rain
you gave us water    we made private lakes
you gave us fireflies and sand dunes    we made single-use cutlery
dung beetles, tree shade,    plastic grass
wild strawberries and kissing    and landfills

you gave us stars    we made stickers
to stick onto our ceilings
to look like stars

## virgins, to the back

*Many of the younger rank and file would have probably arrived in France as virgins . . . the low hanging fruits combined with the apparent certainty of their imminent death offered tempting pickings.*

– https://historycollection.com/dont-know-intimacy-world-war/

*Even the full Monty of trench warfare couldn't numb him to the surprise of seeing such a long queue outside the establishment, which he likened to a scene from a football match back in Old Blighty.*

– https://historycollection.com/dont-know-intimacy-world-war/

before each battle, brothel queues were busiest
'tempting pickings' (also known as women, mainly illiterate)
waited in cramped bedrooms, all welcome-smile and bosom

the likelier death was, the more young men shuffled forwards
three hundred per woman each night before the somme
lined up outside the lights for a final touch   or first touch   or both

butter scrounged for lube to quell vaginal hell-fire rubbing
trench foot, rum and syphilis,
condoms denied everyone except the officers

married men sent to the front, 'virgin' boys sent to the back
mud-stuck shoelaces unravelling into more stuck mud
awkward taunts to young ones         *go on lad!*

young women's bodies offered up like priests aside a dying bed
young men's bodies offered up like flags jammed into frozen fields
lick the salty taste of tears before barbed wire and whistles

*stranger, hold me close*
*please, don't speak of death yet*

how many final comforts were sought
in the bodies of these 'temptresses'
beds bare as trenches                    unmedalled, unmentioned

before somewhere in the distance
another bomb   another boy bleeding
another letter opened   another mother screaming

## bastard

man-made label
for a baby
newborn palms
tiny as marigold
and butterflies

your mother's milk
still runs, yes
unmarried breasts
do not differentiate
such bully labels

sleep now,
let me sniff
your newborn skin
smells how
heaven should

**virginity, loss**

*or the ongoing obsession with purity,*
*as defined by strangers who know nothing about your life*

do not tell me when i lost it, you weren't there –
not the first time, nor the second,
nor any other moment when innocence inside me
splintered and sunk

do not tell me which moments have changed me,
your rules were never my body

i lost nothing the night i pulled him inside me,
nineteen and kissing, excitedly twitching
toes into toes into shell-shattered sands

yet the day a grown man pressed his cold adult hand
soft on the flat of my back as we posed for a photograph
fifteen and frozen, i felt innocence flood from my flesh
like kittens thrown weighted in rivers

do not tell me when i lost it
i have lost it now over and over
restored and restolen

five years old, bawling,
boys beating our dog with a stick
as she whimpered, chained up and begging,
blood mingled with laughter
as mum clutched my tiny hand tighter
fighting them off

do not tell us what is rot and what is blossom
we know when we have blossomed, and when we rot

the world is brimful with purity-shattered –
each hand uninvited, the jolt
of each ambulance siren, footsteps
of unceasing strangers, drones targeting
hospital cots from distant computers,
the death of each child, the death
of each person you love

do not tell me which touches
have mattered the most,
this is your obsession, not mine

one life-changing minute
when the make-believe virgin inside us
sparkles or sins

this world is a show full of wonder and horror
your scriptures were never my skin

**today, no one dies**

no ice thick enough, ungritted on slippy pavements
for accidental falls, no bones fatally broken,
no cold so cold it slows blood to freezing point in doorways,
no heating bills too high, no d.i.y. gone wrong,
no mould spread into lungs by unpunished landlord negligence,
no avalanche, at least not where any fingers cling,
no final breaths, no last goodbyes, no hunger strikes,
no *such a shames*, no *far too youngs*, no *surely nots*,
no sudden catastrophic fights, no panicked knives in stomachs,
no lovers blamed and beaten over football matches,
no trains delayed by too much sorrow on the tracks,
no car crash, no hymen checks, no cot death, no stillborn,
no honour chokes, no overdose, no back streets,
no coat-hangers, no cross-fire, no house fire, no warfare,
no faulty wires, no faulty brakes, no faulty fairground rides –
just life. please, today, just life.

# CHAPTER TWO

## *Making Shame: Hell is Where the Hemline is*

CHARLOTTE CHURCH: *I didn't internalise it. I just knew it was fucking wrong.*
TOMMY TIERNAN: *What do you think was being sold?*
CHARLOTTE CHURCH: *Innocence, innocence was being sold.*

– RTÉ ONE, interview on the *Tommy Tiernan Show*

*You may not control all the events that happen to you, but you can decide not to be reduced by them.*

– MAYA ANGELOU

As a small child, I loved Peperami; that processed chewy meat stick thing that comes in a tight condom-like wrapper. I stopped eating them when I was still little, as I found out how meat was made and freaked out.

I don't remember when I began begging not to eat meat but my mum says I was about five or six. My favourite toys at the time were a farmyard set, My Little Pony and a new plastic Flounder from *The Little Mermaid* McDonald's Happy Meal. I was so upset at the idea of eating any of these beloved toys. None of my family are or ever have been vegetarian, and my parents kindly gave in to my pleas after a year or so of pretending mince was made of beans. I also stopped eating mushrooms because I somehow convinced myself they were tortoises' feet.

One of the few things I missed were the Peperami sticks. I would often take one to my room and sniff the wrapper, sometimes taking it out of the packet and sniffing that too. The smell of the spices was so delicious, unlike any other food I ate.

Years later I picked up a Peperami packet and read that one of the ingredients was 150 per cent pork. Mathematically, it threw me; poetically, I love it.

When I had my first child, this Peperami label kept coming back into my head.

My body had expanded and filled up with another human being, belly bulging like a hamster sneaking treats into its cheeks. I looked in the mirror the week before I gave birth; my own body with another body inside it. I was over 100 per cent body.

Birth pushed me to extremes I never knew possible; screams of wonder and worry filling a tiny crowded hospital room as my daughter and I separated, extraordinary, sore, in awe. Every feeling was a fairground, up and down, roller-coaster roaring, exaggerated a thousand times over in blinking neon lights and whirring engines, constantly climbing, fearful of potential unexpected descents.

I know not everybody feels love rushing through the minute they gaze at a newborn and there are so many reasons for this, but I did. Giving birth was the most difficult thing I hope to do in my life, but it went as smoothly as it could, we were lucky, and when I looked at my daughter it was in utter love-guzzling amazement and terror at her fragility.

I left the hospital, and visitors flocked. The baby ate and screamed and cried and slept. I did the same, minus the screaming and sleeping. On about the third night, she slept for nearly an hour and a half straight. Visitors had left. Her dad was exhausted, finally asleep. The world all around me was way past its bedtime. I wasn't crying. The stars were out. My daughter was content in my arms, eyes closed, tiny lungs rising and falling. The world felt newer than I'd ever known. Newer than new. And more silent than silence.

I sat in the stillness, staring at her face.

My gran once described the silence after air raids as akin to the silence when a screaming baby finally slept soundly, hoping that the peace might last a little longer each time.

Staring at a baby's sleeping face for hours in silent darkness was not something I had ever done before and the more I did it, the more thoughts rushed in; some gorgeous, some gruesome.

The central thought I had was of innocence; this tiny face, tiny heart, tiny mouth and toes, totally reliant on others to guide it into life; purity personified. It broke my heart.

Firstly, for those unheld by loving arms. Secondly, for those who could have been and were forcibly removed from such a cuddle. My stomach became constantly sick with any society, culture, religion that has ever deemed a baby such as this, sleeping as the stars silently blinked through the windows, as bad or shameful or sinful.

In school, we had discussed various Christian beliefs related to the afterlife. Unbaptised babies, would they be allowed into heaven? was one such discussion. We learnt about limbo. I twitched as pins and needles now crept up my cradle of arms. The whole idea of this disgusted me more than ever before.

A tired new mum, twenty-seven, trying my best, unmarried, a healthy baby now snoring sweetly, me still bleeding from birth, full of more love than I'd ever known, whilst knowing too that if I were in another place or time, in another family even, this most gorgeous peace, baby snuggled into my skin, could be viewed with utter contempt, disgust, shame, despite everyone being healthy and loved. In so many places and pasts, my baby would have been ripped from my arms. In many, I would have been locked up.

I thought of the story we'd heard of the Virgin Mary from a young age, how we'd been taught that she was the purest of the pure; the peak of holy. She was the most famous mum I knew of besides Tina Turner. I do not believe in the immaculate conception, but of course, I wasn't there, so can't know for sure. What I do know are the effects that this ideal of the virgin, of holy motherhood, of purity and conception and marriage, has had on so many other mothers and their families, both women in my own family and those unknown to me.

If I had given birth to my daughter when my grandmother gave birth to my mother, I dread to think what could have happened to my body, my baby, my family.

I am truly done with belief systems that seek to shame pregnancy and motherhood, uphold damaging and sometimes murderous ideas of purity and innocence, or which question newborn babies as anything other than the helpless innocent wee brutes they are. I do not believe in a Christian heaven, I don't know what I believe in, but if I did, babies and children would be unquestionably in alongside all the unmarried women who died abandoned due to childbirth.

The day I gave birth, I felt like a newborn myself. Desperate for love and assistance. The earth had shifted its axis and I had to re-learn how to stand up and navigate it all with another human being clinging to me, drinking from my body. Literally too – I had no idea how to stand up and walk whilst holding a baby. A few hours after the birth, still lying in the hospital bed with a baby on my chest, I was told to get up as I had to change rooms. I had to ask someone to show me how to stand up and walk with a baby on my chest.

There is another definition of the word virgin, a more general concept: a person who is inexperienced in a given activity or field. I like this definition; everyone is a virgin in so many ways and 'losing your virginity' in this sense just means learning new things, becoming more knowledgeable in a specific area of life.

At my first poetry reading, the organiser of the night asked if I had ever done a reading before. I said no. He introduced me onto the stage (a little space at the front of the café) as a poetry virgin and, as I was about to start reading, an older woman shouted from the back: *she doesn't look like a virgin!* and everybody laughed, including me.

When I became a mother, in this newbie sense of the word, I felt like the biggest virgin I ever had; a total virgin mother; a virgin human. I felt as newborn as the newborn in my arms.

I have decided that this meaning of virgin is the only meaning I will now give any credence to; someone who is new to something. The other definition, the one which holds up first time intercourse as some pinnacle of holy judgement, I've had quite enough of; as a mother, as a woman, as a human. I will not be passing it on to the next generation.

Oh, and Peperami. According to the pack: 'Made with 37.5g pork per 25g finished product, as some moisture is lost during curing and drying.'

## call me

even if you're in the wrong place at the wrong time
with a full moon and a lone wolf
whimpering bloody-pawed from your insides;
if you are knee-deep, puddle-spilled
puking up every warning that i gave you, just call me –
i will pick you up quick as prayers leave lips
i have blankets and hot chocolate, arms locked open,
i do not care what you have done,
never let shame stop you reaching for your phone
and dialling my number; i am no god  i am no judge
i am your mother – call me and i will come

**hell is where the hemline is**

*for anyone who has had their school skirt measured*

she held the ruler to their thighs
as if heaven were a measurement
            you'd think we could have sorted this by now

tell the truth: kids, the world is a wolf den
but it is easier to blame you for the sharp edge of their teeth
            my grandmother was thirteen the first time

beatings dependent on inch of flesh *on show*
between the hemline and the devil
            same wooden ruler used for both

taller girls stood no chance
nor those with longer legs or larger backsides
            my mum was almost six foot

my own shorter frame did not absolve me
from teachers' tutting and detentions, measuring,
measuring
            at least, no beatings then

today, almost a century has passed
since your great grandmother was lined up
            yet here we are,

rushing breakfast, driving you in early
so that a grown-up may squat before your crotch
            three fingers held together

to measure the length of flesh seen
between your kneecaps and your school skirt
before the bell tolls,

before the bell tolls once again

**dressed like that**

we were excited to get boobs
balanced apples in our bras
to see how we would feel when we were *women*

we tried on dresses our mothers wore
when leaving late at night
or when crisps were put in bowls

pink lipstick on our lips, we laughed,
held fashion shows in overgrown high heels
checked our shimmies in the mirror

the main thing i remember was the fun of it –
how thrilling, imagining our bodies growing into bodies
like the bodies of people doing things we couldn't

the world, a giant party that awaited us,
we giggled,
practising our pirouettes and pouts

and everybody smiled,
until we tried to leave the house

**when my daughter wears a top that shows her belly, and we leave the house**

oh sorry, did you not get the memo?
we're not doing that any more

that thing,
where you scan my daughter's outfit, then frown at me,
as if i would not dive in front of buses, turn a dagger
dutifully into the groin of any creep who tried to leap

raise your eyebrows that high
and they might just fly away

i know, i know, you're only trying to be protective,
(it has never been protective) or perhaps you're not,

either way, it is summer and it is hot
and it is neither her fault nor mine
that shorts are designed shorter for girls, by adults
and tops are designed tighter for girls, by adults
and it took centuries of protest to change laws
allowing men to marry teenage girls, and children,
then legally rape them

the day a stranger grabbed my breasts
through my open car window
i was in my purple woolly jumper

your friend was in pyjamas
your friend was in a tracksuit
your friend was in a swimsuit
your friend was in a football strip
your friend was in school uniform

your friend was in a burka
your friend was in a ballgown
your friend was in a babygro
your friend was in a coffin

so go on, roll your eyes back to where they came from
it must hurt to scowl so hard

tutting at teenage girls in miniskirts and short dresses
will not rid the world of rapists, it will only strain your face

do you remember in our grandmas' days
when ladies never swore, skirts worn far below the knees,
and no one ever hurt them?

**peacock**

often, i undressed at the window
curtains dishevelled as if mistakenly open
hoping he might notice from his room across the street
*look up now!* glimpse the softness of my unassuming skin

*we dress for no one but ourselves!* you yell

cool, but what of those who do? strutting, parading,
all butterfly-patterned, peacock-bodied,
pouting-orchid-faced; dressing to be desired
is not mutually exclusive with deserving to be safe

sometimes we all want proof we're still opaque,

and sometimes, after months untouched
when skin feels more museum vase than living blood
the loose wool of my jumper has uncovered
a globe of golden shoulder to a passing, glancing stranger,

and yes, i wonder, if they might think of it again,

take it home, caress it like a turtle shell,
closed-eyed, polish the oval edges
and i drift, a little bolstered, a little seen,
toes peeking just outside the sheets

## just a penis to practise on was all i wanted

not a lover's or a creep's, just someone
who could kindly lend me theirs
for the afternoon or a few weeks or forever
just a penis, detached from the owner
blu-tacked to my dressing table
next to the hairbrush with my name engraved
and my orange neon markers
just a penis i could look at for a while
once i'd finished all my revision
work out its particulars without offending anyone
how to hold it in my palms,
how to ease the foreskin back
without snapping any ligaments
there were stories of boys bleeding, screams
fists gripped so recklessly in first fumbled wanks
the banjo snapped and never played again
i did not want to hurt anyone
and i did not enjoy being bad at things
especially in front of the person
i was hoping to impress   infuriating, really,
this inability to practise before the test
until i realised boys were human too
and they all liked different bands,
and touch is not a maths exam, and i didn't have a dressing table

## the comments beneath the video on pornhub are gorgeous

tear emojis mostly, lamentations, confessions from anonymous grown men: *fuck, i'm lonely*, writes *bigdick88*. others nod hearts back in open brackets. it is morning and *bonniealex* are waking up in bed. they assure us they are lovers in real life. the search was *real couple real sex*. so tiring, the theatres of flesh. they cuddle as they kiss. his testicles squished snug against her butt cheeks. *i miss this so bad*, writes *wetcock42*. *where did it go?* replies *uselessnoone123*. their soft dough-bodies merge belly into breast. a wide-angle lens shows his penis enter timelessly. he grasps her folds of flesh as if the edge of unknown earth. *my soul hurts* types *milfmunch69*. they begin to slow spoon as if slow spooning were the remedy for everything; the world is watching, secretly from bedrooms, wiping cum and tears on tissues, rubbing cocks and clits. *if each day began this way, war would not exist – hornyjordie83*. *ticklemyarsehole61* hard agrees*

---

* comments taken from online; usernames have been altered but kept on theme with the originals

**sending nudes**

*dear sons, dear daughters,*

if one day, you decide to share
a snapshot of your body
stripped autumn bare (because
they asked you and you want to
and you feel certain that you do)
please know, i will not judge you
nor think any less of you
        your body is your body,
            i've sent such photos too

but if one day, that person
you've shared your photos with
abuses your skin's secrets
shares it, shows it, shames it
declares you slag or slut for it
mocks you with their friends
tries to bribe you into more
tries to stop you seeking help
please know, i will not judge you
nor love you any less
        try not to feel ashamed
            all blame lies with them

your body is your body
to do with as you please
and photographs of autumn
will never capture all the colours
of the dancing, golden leaves
just please be careful, and remember,

any photograph you send
with one touch of a button
could be shared with *anyone*,
and please remember
        that some people,
                *are* cunts

**in loving memory of the kissing tree**

the pale green leaves of the common hawthorn
are often the first to appear each spring
and there we were, almost summer, almost eleven
sunbrellaed by the low white blossom

it took three trips to the tree till i was certain
he smiled each time i shook my head
carved a compass heart in bark instead

for some, it is the may tree,
nicknamed for the month it bloomed
for us, it was the kissing tree, love-shrine
to lips on lips in the woods inside our school

the second time, petal-confetti blessings,
lips ready, i turned my head *'no, sorry'*
*'don't worry'* he kissed me on the cheek instead

these blossoms were once banned, spring garlands
made for may day celebrations judged unholy crowns
to carnal love by those in power; how strange,
the things we've had forbidden – such fear of flowers

it has been said that the hawthorn
is an unlucky plant to bring into a house;
then again, so much has been said

the third time *yes* he checks again *yes,*
*yes* my mouth pressed against his mouth
a softness i still feel
each time the hawthorn bloom is out

my lips are layered now
with many years of grateful kissing
like paintings   painted over paintings

about that first kiss, i don't remember much –
how many seconds we pressed our lips together,
but afterwards, he whispered *'thank you,
thank you very much'*

and set the bar, at ten, forever

**never, as in not once, ever?**

the nurse asks if there's any possibility you are pregnant you giggle turn to your mum grin tick no still the adult themes are set your friend starts her periods at nine a smiling adult tells her she's *a woman now* she vomits soon after you stop swimming too *tampons are not for virgins*, a smiling adult tells you you listen it will not be the last time the dentist asks if there's *any possibility you are pregnant* you smile say *no* the doctor asks if there's *any possibility you are pregnant* you say *no* the nurse asks if you are *sexually active* you wonder why the question has changed your friend has a period so heavy the gym pants (only) the girls have to do sport in cannot contain it the doctor suggests *the contraceptive pill* her parents don't let her take it *she's not a slut* you are lucky you bleed lightly but you are nervous wearing the white sports kit for tennis you wonder why so many sports clothes must be white the doctor asks if you are *sexually active* you're not sure if that includes fingering you reply *no*, end it like a question at the counter to buy the morning after pill the man asks *when did you last have intercourse* you say *never* you say you're *just being careful* you feel like an idiot the nurse asks what *contraception* you are on you say *condoms* you say *combined pill* you say *headaches* you say *oestrogen only* you say *occasional intermittent bleeding* you ask what *normal pain* is they say *everything* you wonder who you're doing this all for // at the first check up after the birth of your daughter the nurse looks at your stitching says *intercourse will probably be ok now probably* she says *probably* she asks what *contraception you're thinking of using* she asks nothing about anything but penetration and contraception you go home you cry your body is still healing you feel worse saying *no* now you book an appointment ask if *the copper coil* is better than *the one with the hormones* it scares you a little to stop your periods entirely it scares you a little to have metal inside your body it scares you a little to have metal without anaesthetic pushed into your uterus // the first night it is in six hours of cramping you imagine the contraption inside you you cry google side effects of the copper coil after two hours of reading it tells you you will die you hear accounts of other women in pain it's ok in the morning the next week it is normal each time you have a stomach ache you wonder if the coil is stuck inside your cervix you wonder if it's working you breathe out each time the blood comes you wonder who you're doing this all for // the nurse says it will be *easier to put another coil in straight away* it has been in for ten years you say you *do not want another coil* you say *you do not want anything in your body for a while just to see what it feels like not to worry* the doctor frowns asks *what contraception* you'll be using you say *cunnilingus* she doesn't laugh it's not a joke though you say *condoms* just to keep things moving the appointment is cancelled for a fourth time covid the iud has been in longer than it should now you're sure it's causing thrush you google *can the coil cause thrush if left in too long* you google *can the coil cause cancer if left in too long* you google *can the coil embed itself into your uterus and then rust and kill you if left in too long* you call again you google how to remove the coil by yourself you google *has anybody died from removing the coil by themselves* you get through to the sexual health clinic the nurse asks you if you can *feel the strings* you try to *feel the strings* you don't know what the *strings* are you hold the phone to your ear with your shoulder as you sit on the bathroom floor two fingers as far into your vagina as they have ever been you are sitting talking to a stranger on the phone with your fingers far into your vagina you feel so stupid you cry you cannot *feel the strings* she says *if you cannot feel the strings you may need to go to hospital* nobody said *hospital* when you had this put inside you you hang up mid-conversation because you are crying again you wash your hands wonder who you're doing this all for // at the doctor you are asked if there's *any* chance you are *pregnant* your daughter on your lap giggles waits in silence for your answer you smile shake your head as confidently as percentages on packets the doctor asks if you are *married* you wonder what difference a wedding contract makes to your vagina the doctor asks what *contraception* you are on your daughter starts to fidget you get a new toy from your bag // you take your daughter to the doctor the form asks if there's any chance she could be pregnant she looks at you and laughs in school uniform you tick no sob into your sleep that night // you meet your friend for lunch you are tired you cry and feel ridiculous you say you are just so tired of all the questions // he looks blank *sorry, what questions?* says he's never once been asked about contraception

**my belly, pregnant**

informed every passer-by that i was not one
moreover, that we hadn't used protection
        on the street of crowded cafés
a stranger points, yelling
skin the scent of settled whisky
declares from loudspeaker lungs, i am
*too fucking young* to have a child
        a nightclub, ten sweating adult palms
rub my belly without asking, turn by turn,
my stretching skin now the statue of a woman
bronze breasts rubbed for luck so much
by groping strangers, the gold shows below,
        arriving into glasgow
grandma jokes again if i'm allowed
on virgin trains these days, the first time
was funnier, she passes me a cardigan
        colleagues discussing yoga
invite me to join them just to make the joke
*seems you already know the downward dog*
        older women in pearl necklaces,
skirts the pattern of bus seats, raise eyebrows,
tut, tut, when i pass them, perhaps my imagination,
        either way, i walk on, waddling,
never more jealous of the men
the men, whose bodies announce nothing

**cool, cool, there's a male contraceptive pill**

sure, it would be nice to pass on the responsibility
like letting my kid wash up the dishes after dinner

**desire**

my body craves you inside it but i am frightened that you have never woken up as the robin starts to sing outside the window, searching, before you've even had a morning coffee, what the different shades of blood might mean, depending, maybe slightly, deeper red, what it might signify, searching just in case, just so you can get on with your day. there are always two pregnancy tests in my knicker drawer for the seconds my brain keeps reminding me of the percentages on the leaflets, *it is never one hundred, hollie.* last night, my period still a little late, i watched a video of the abortion pill process till two am, read reports of the pain or not pain, checked clinics and mailbox delivery, got lost in news reports of laws obliterated in the u.s.a., wondered what i would do in their place if, imagine, imagine. i start imaginary conversations with you, i ask *would you be ok never inside me again? only oral sex and fingering? if it happens here, i mean, would you be ok never entering my body* and i smile to your imaginary concern, comforting *ofcourse, ofcourse.* the conversation runs inside my head like drilling in the middle of the city, i feel guilty at this daydream. i cry at the idea of not pleasing you enough. perhaps, i think, it would be best to just to break up with you before you break up with me once i cancel intercourse because i cannot take the pressure of perhaps. it isn't the same with a condom, says the grown man on the podcast. it isn't the same when you are petrified of getting pregnant and potentially dying without access to healthcare, i reply. he doesn't hear me. perhaps we should just watch romcoms and masturbate a lot. i cry at the thought of our imaginary break up, i cry at the idea of those early months afterwards without you, unable to concentrate on anything but you, seeing your face in my cereal every morning, unable to wank anyway because of the sadness. i cry at the idea of the sadness without you. i cry at how heavy it feels in my body making decisions other people are making for me. i cry at the thought of getting pregnant in a country where politicians laugh as pregnancy might kill me. i cry at an imaginary miscarriage in the toilets at work, passing out next to the second cubicle with blood running through the cotton of my tights, then being arrested for murder. i check my pants again, a small patch of unexpected red, i search 'spotting' on the internet, wondering if this is my period finally starting or perhaps a sign of pregnancy or cancer or the clotting side effect i read about in the leaflets for the combination of oestrogen and progestogen pills. i know, i know it's not your fault you have never woken up sweating, mid-dream, wondering whether the soreness in my breasts is a side effect of the injection or its failings. i imagine being pregnant again, i imagine the man laughing in the street at my pregnant body again. i wonder what insults i would get this time now i am an older mum not a younger mum. i check the pill packet again, i check the condoms, i check the rhythm method, i check the calendar, i check my sanity. it's not your fault, i know, but just once or maybe twice or maybe every first sunday of the new moon i would like you in my womb, worrying, i would like all men inside my womb, worrying, i would like all of the senators and all of the judges and the father and the son and the holy spirit to sit inside my womb as i wander around my bedroom wondering if the swelling in my belly, in my breasts, in my brain, will be bothered to vote in the next election, i would like them all with me in my womb at the next election, in my bedroom, in the bathroom, in the shower, as i see it, the blood, the blood, i see it, just a little later than expected, running from my insides like my own ribbons of freedom, thanking god, although i don't believe in god, that it is red and it is real and it is here.

**or maybe, finally, just mary?**

across the country, beneath christmas lights
five-year-olds dress up as mary, the virgin one
her name rolls from kiddy tongues
easy as crayons and playtime

we could just call her mary? no-one says
exclude her sexual status from her name?
a bit embarrassing for the young girl, perhaps?
did they call her virgin mary at the time?

did the three men, arriving awkwardly
with perfume for a child, write: *for virgin mary
and joseph* on the card, or *virgin mary
and virgin joseph*, and did she, mary, in turn

call them *the three wise men* or *the three men*
or did she actually know their names? or perhaps
she was too busy giving birth to baby jesus
to hear them wander in; imagine

if we did the same to everyone, our first names
all drum-rolled by our most significant sexual experience:
*cunnilingus christopher, never-been-fingered lina,
cums-more-easily-with-a-handy-than-penetration barry*

what would the costumes be? would tired parents
stay up until three am sewing bedsheets into tunics
for the *asexual shepherd* and his *mating-season sheep*?
and once jesus was born,

and mary was officially allowed intercourse
(i assume) after that, if there was a play about her life
beyond that birth, her life at thirty or sixty-five
that primary school pupils put on for parents,

would they still have to call her *virgin mary*
or *mary-previously-known-as-virgin-mary*
or *not-a-virgin-now-but-was-a-virgin-when-*
*she-gave-birth-to-jesus-mary*, or maybe  finally

# CHAPTER THREE

## *Making Memories: Life, Pre-loved*

*Centuries of pleasure before us and after us,*
*still right now, a softness like the worn fabric of a nightshirt*

– ADA LIMÓN, *Lover*

*If I didn't define myself for myself,*
*I would be crunched into other people's fantasies for me*
*and eaten alive.*

– AUDRE LORDE

I was thinking about love. Then touch. What makes it special. What makes it feel so good sometimes. Then, I thought about the phrase 'saving yourself' and how many times I heard this phrase, either in real life or on screens, when romance started to become physical.

Not in the general sense of the word. Not in the 'go! save yourself!' stay-alive sense, but in the more sexual sense, used most commonly in phrases like 'I'm saving myself for marriage.'

I find it weird we have this one phrase which in one sense defines 'yourself' as your whole self, your whole entire life, but which in the other defines 'yourself' solely as sexual intercourse, or more bluntly, your genitals, and always in relation to someone else; for marriage, for a husband, for 'the one'. We were never told to 'save ourselves' until we ourselves were ready; saving yourself for yourself sort of thing.

I understand people wanting to wait, it should be your choice what specific physical or mental experiences you want to share with who and when and with what religious or governmental blessing/certification. I just find the phrase a bit strange, because in one scenario, if you don't 'save yourself', you literally die. In the other, if you don't 'save yourself', you've had sexual intercourse. Those are two very different things.

I realise that the phrase can also be used about food. As in, 'no, I won't have any more mashed potato, thanks, I'm saving myself for pudding', but I didn't think about that when I wrote these poems. Saying that, there is quite a lot about food in this bit of the book because food plays a massive role in my love (of) life.

Nowadays, after centuries of struggling for bodily autonomy, many more people can make their own decisions about what intimate experiences they want or don't want to save. Lovely. But I was looking up the history of all this saving yourself in terms of marriage and virginity, and unsurprisingly, it was all pretty property related.

No, it was not dreamt up by two warm-hearted lovers who thought it would be a glorious romantic gesture, but instead was instilled by those in power during times when a wife was quite literally, legally, a possession passed from father to husband. So, a woman – or girl, really – who had already been penetrated, whether consensually or through rape, was deemed damaged goods. From this sprung traditions such as (medically debunked) virginity testing, as well as the infamous (also medically debunked) bedsheet blood checks.

In certain times and places, even having been kissed by another (family excluded) or having shown your ankles to another, was enough to stamp a big red label on the packet; the packet being a person.

I was thinking about all that: person as possession, power, this enduring fixation with someone needing to be yours and yours alone. Certified. New. No previous owner. No previous experience.

And then I thought about products that don't have heartbeats and feelings and how similar obsessions with newness and untouched have also been pushed on us by those in power. And then I started thinking about my grandma's clothes.

In the relatively small amount of time between my grandma's young adult life and my own, the number of new products pushed on people, produced cheaply to be mass purchased, has exploded. Whereas my gran had clothes she would keep all her adult life, darning socks, cloth bags for shopping, a Sunday best for church or dances, maybe three at a push, often passed down from older siblings, we now have companies pushing narratives of single-use clothing, single-use bags, single-use cups and plates and so on. Use it and throw it. Everything new.

Then I thought of porn, and this programme I watched about the industry of finding young people, mainly teenage girls, hiring them for a season and then ditching them, because viewers want new bodies to watch.

Then I thought of all the dating apps, swiping past people like sweeties, paper bag in your hand and a gold coin to spend.

Then I thought about 'body count' interviews increasingly popping up on my social media feed.

For those who don't know, these are supposedly light-hearted interviews, mainly outside nightclubs or on shopping streets, mainly, from what I see, by young straight men to other young straight men (no other category of human seems quite so bothered about adult sexual experience) where these men are asked about their ideal 'body count'; ideal body count being the number of other sexual partners a woman could have had to still be deemed 'good enough' for them to consider dating. 'Wife material'-type chat. Yes, women also talk about body count, it just seems to be certain straight men who give the most shit about the numbers.

The thing with the body-count concept – putting aside for a moment the re-inventing of these age-old tropes around purity – is that they are mathematically ridiculous.

This question of 'body count' (fuck, that phrase is truly horrendous) is never about how much sex these (mainly) women have had, not how many actual times she's had sex or how experienced she is sexually nor how safe that sex was (which really should be the sole concern of any new partner) but purely the number of *different* sexual partners she has had, by which we are mainly talking intercourse. Bluntly, how many other men's penises have been inside her for her to still be worthy of these young nightclub-goers.

It is the same ludicrous mathematics fostered for years in discussions about 'loose' women. When people talk of 'loose' women, they are referring to the idea that a woman's vagina will magically loosen the more different men she has slept with, but weirdly it will magically *not loosen* in a woman who has continuously shagged only one man, especially if that man is you. Especially if you are married. Marital sex does not cause loose vaginas, no matter how much of it you have. Either way, they are highly overestimating penis size and underestimating the elasticity of most vaginal canals.

Whatever reason some people continue to fear, dislike, judge, feel insecure about a partner's previous sexual experience, these questions are mathematical nonsense. Even if someone has a very low 'body count' they may still be extremely experienced sexually. Even if someone has had intercourse once, they may be carrying three sti's. Even if someone has never had a single sexual partner, they may be a whizz with their fingers. Oh yeah, we shame masturbation too. Urgh.

Back to clothes.

Recently, second-hand shops, or used goods shops, have been using the phrase 'pre-loved', which turns this whole idea on its head. How gorgeous to have something in your life already loved by others; something with a past, a story, experience, knowledge; something to treasure for exactly that reason. Something which doesn't need to be new to be new.

And then I thought of love again and the loves of those loves I've known who taught them about love and loving before they then loved me.

So that's where my brain was when I wrote these poems; flicking through thoughts of pre-loved clothing, body-count videos, romance, repeated soppy experiences, sofas squished to the shape of your butt cheeks, and single-use plastic bags.

And my gran's butter dish, which makes memories of her reappear every time I use it. Like a genie, in a butter dish. Magic.

## second-hand bookshops are the lovers of the world

*I do love second-hand books that open to the page*
*some previous owner read oftenest*

– HELENE HANFF

the books in here
have all been held before
lover-soft alluring
fingered in bath tubs
and on beach towels,
rushed to bed
for early winter nights
words wandering by lamplight
into dreamers' minds
as they have wandered
into dreamers' minds before,
each eager set of eyes
treasuring new pleasures
and if you're lucky
some markings in the margin
a dedication to a loved one
pages folded and unfolded
at corners to come back to
a love heart sketched in pencil
next to another lover's
favourite line
you might otherwise
have missed

## ~~secondhand~~ lover, pre-loved

~~i pray~~ every lover ~~i~~/you have is pre-loved ~~or else what?~~
~~slab of raw~~ heart beating ~~bloody and~~ love~~less~~,
~~as midwives rush long, empty corridors~~
~~for someone to swaddle and sing them to sleep~~

~~yes, i pray every lover has known hope~~
~~in the hold of another, skin~~ warming their skin
like cafés at christmas, fairylit fingers,
bones cloaked with blankets,
mulled wine made of their hot scarlet blood

~~unafraid of~~ belting the lyrics to love songs
with the windows rolled down ~~yes~~
~~i pray every lover is~~ notebook and pen
ink-full of stories to tell ~~me~~

~~stop panicking,~~
~~there are always more pages to fill –~~
~~feel the heat on the nape of your neck~~
~~no less glorious for yesterday's sun~~

keep?

~~wise to the wonders~~
~~our soft human hearts have to offer;~~
touching ~~my~~/your lips like a bowl full of cherries,
already knowing how sweet this could be

**the mathematics of body count**

*after watching another video of a young man interviewing three other young men discussing how many lovers their futures wives are allowed to have had*

*no more than two bruv* he declares, and the others nod *yeah yeah*
as if a matter of national security how many specific separate penises
a potential girlfriend may already have loved inside her skin.
oh straight guys outside the nightclub, why do you obsess so much
over other straight guys' penises? nudging one another
like muddled, horny toddlers, as the girls, already dancing
happy around their handbags await your crucial moral judgement.
what is it you're against? her experience? her vagina? her pleasure?
are you afraid she might compare you to other lovers?
expect more from your encounter? do you not realise that a woman
with a body count of one may still have had more sex
than another woman after fifty one-night stands? or is just
the specific number of penises you're after? do fingers matter?
cunnilingus? masturbation? will you ask about those too
with your big boy clipboard and your tick box? is there a limit on her kissing?
can her lips be too knowledgeable for your liking? oh young man
obsessed with penises that came before him, do you not know that women,
however many men they've previously let inside their bodies
for whatever length of time, all have hands at the end of their arms
with which they are potentially very dextrous at making themselves
orgasm; and that even women with no sexual experience, nothing
to compare you to, your perfect *wife material*, holy body count of zero,
not one single other penis having ever touched their skin,
can still spot a dickhead when they see one

## 'saving yourself'

ought to be about life-vests in your lungs
pull the toggle to inflate your self esteem
see the lights lining the darkness
check the exits, clearly marked
so if one day you find yourself
plummeting from skies towards a life
too cold to cope with, you will remember
there are lifeboats you can swim to
a whistle to attract attention
already on that string around your neck
like a locket full of cries for help
my love, as loud as you are able, blow it
blow it again, believe, someone is coming

the world is better with you in it

breathe in,
let your flesh inflate,

and float

## the *other living room*

the *other living room* in grandma's house was forever ready for the vicar or the queen; museum-mannered, out of bounds to children's clumsy games;* polished coffee table forbidden land to any actual coffee cups; immortal fake lilies gasping in glass pebbles beside the fruit bowl filled with plastic polished oranges and apples

the sofa in the *other living room* was pillow-plump, cushions matched, so much snugger than the tight-lipped wooden chairs we sat on in the front room sipping soup never served in the gold-rimmed bowls kept high up in glass cabinets next to the dishes shaped like shells we never ate our hobnobs off, saved for special guests who never came, silver spoons still wedding-fresh in purple velvet coffins, *just in case*, one day, *just in case*, suddenly, the vicar, or the queen

cross-legged, i would fidget on the rug amongst the grown-ups, inhaling chat of newspapers and crosswords, gazing keenly across the peacock-patterned carpet of the hallway which separated us from *the other living room*, inexplicably empty, where i would occasionally sneak to, escaping unseen on all fours to run my fingers through the thick woollen grasses of the carpet, starfish flat against its softness, inhale the ever-scented-newness of the triple-seated sofa undented by daily buttocks, and the piano, shiny as a conker, and the fireplace, forever dusted, never lit

* my cousin Tracy just told me she was allowed in gran's other room anytime, and that they always used to play in there, so maybe it was just me

## blockbuster video stores

for your sleepover, you ask if you might watch a real dvd
like a *real one*  do we have them?  can you choose one?
it's a meagre selection
still, it seems like you want to touch something

music is ghost now; coins do not clinkle in pockets
no sprint to the record shops, rush for the newest release
no art on the covers to covet

i tell you how listening to entire new albums
was like devouring a book, cover to cover on sundays
flat out on your carpet, eyes to the ceiling
no click as you lower the needle now
snap close the cassette till it skips or the tape lace unrolls

fuck, nothing breaks any more

you ask me again about blockbuster video stores
as if a tale of the ancients

i tell you of parents, tapping their watches
none of the films you wanted to rent are left on the shelves
each dvd scratched halfway through
popcorn, and a bottle of coke if you're lucky

you inhale, as if the closure of blockbuster video stores
were akin to the fall of the wall in berlin
in silence, you flick through our old dvds
like playing the keys of an ancient piano
salvaged from shipwreck

i show you photos of grandma out dancing
dressed in the same dress each week,

you ask me what sunday best means

**over and over again**

one weekend dress for dancing in, a sunday best for church
one outfit to look good in, the other to look *good* in

prayers and parties, washed on mondays
each week repeating fabrics until no amount of darning

could restitch the two-step tears; how did we go from her
to this? fabric mountains, flailing fish, landfills overspilling,

billionaires convincing us our clothing must be new for every outing
as if the dancing will be livelier with different shoes each week;

who started myths like this? clothes are not the centrepiece,
they never were, the people are, the music – and yes, of course

she begged her mother to cut another from the curtains,
and perhaps she had a third dress then, as her mother rolled her eyes,

her mother, who had one dress, and still waltzed with every suitor
whose hand outstretched to hers, or else chatting by the chairs

with friends she'd known for years, in dresses they had all worn before,
where the jokes were just as funny in pearls passed down from

mothers' mothers' mothers
as the band played all their favourite songs,

## i know exactly what you mean

you send a photo of your breakfast, and i love you
i send a photo of my breakfast back to you –
in the past, perhaps a letter, but now it's pear
cut into pieces beside a slice of toast and butter,
i know exactly what you mean

and in the evenings, my mum would bring
a plate of cut up apple and a pile of salty crisps
and in my bedroom, with my homework
laid out across the carpet, i would thank her
and i would eat it, and she loved me, and i knew it

now it's me who leaves a cup of tea and biscuit
in my daughter's room, and each day after school
we say nothing for an hour but the plate is always clean,
and i always make more dinner in case my friend pops in
for tea, and so does she, and we all know what we mean

and if you were here tonight, i'd cook and you'd wash up –
for now, a selfie of you twirling some spaghetti is enough
and later, before bed, i will take her up some supper
and i remember how gran used to sneak us in
a nighttime treat, as we sat next to each other

on the armchairs, watching tv, drinking warm milk
mixed with brandy, and she would pass me
two tiny squares of chocolate from the plate,
and i always knew exactly what she meant

**at waverley,**

you wait for me
on platform six or platform nine
freckles on your eyelids
fervour in your eyes

at waverley, you've waited now
in snowfall, blossom, sun
smiling behind the barrier
as my train pulls gently in

and when autumn, once more berry-ripe,
flaunts its frosted purple sheen
how i hope you'll be there
waiting, at waverley, again

my nose pressed to the window
as the engines simmer down
station blurred with frantic footsteps
searching faces in the crowds

until i single out the glint of you
pebble-skimmed on sunlit loch
and you smile, and take my heavy bag
as we work out once more how to touch

at waverley, where you wait for me
on platform six or platform nine
freckles on your eyelids
fervour in the skies

waving from the barrier
as my train doors flutter open
ready to turn the day
into a poem

**seduction over a morning fruit bowl**

as i place this purple grape very slowly inside my mouth
like my friend said she did in a mindful eating workshop once –
ancient buddhist knowledge which i'm now mis-using
to try to seduce you, hoping that, watching me across the breakfast table,
you will think, not of this grape, but of my body, and how
desperate you are to learn everything you can about it
before you die, and as i press my teeth, finally, gently
into the thin violet membrane and stare at you across the table the way
actors like juliette binoche and angela bassett and monica bellucci
do so exquisitely, that you will have the sudden urge to rise up
from that chair, bang your hands flat against the wooden surface,
declaring loudly how sorry you are but you simply must go,
and you will push your plate aside and come kiss me
as if inside my mouth were the last lick of maple syrup
from the final maple still alive on planet earth and you will fling
your coat like a cape across your shoulders and i will sit
bewildered as you exit, the door slam echoing for hours after,
wondering where you must be going with such impatience
as you race breathless and bursting, searching the streets
for the nearest yoni massage centre, where you will enrol
in a night class for four days every week after work
and spend the next three years studying, begging me to let you
practise all the new techniques you're learning on my body
and i'll say things like *oh i've got so much work to do tonight, love*
and you'll be like, *but i've already laid the blankets out*
*by the fire and warmed the oils in my hands* and you'll show me
your palms dripping with a combination of coconut and despair
and i'll say *ok fine, but only for two hours today, seriously,*
*because last week you took nearly four and i really do*
*need to get my taxes done* and you'll beg me, beg me
for just a little longer because this week you learnt a new

vulva massage technique using a combination of three fingers,
a feather and your left kneecap to delicately fold my labia
into an origami swan as you whisper incantations sweet into my ears
like perfume in the air from jasmine grown across bridges over rivers
and i'll be like *ok, ok, stop insisting, jeez, fine, i'll do it*
and i'll lie down on the blankets, and let you,
for the third time that week, remove each battery from each clock,
close the curtains, unbutton all my clothing until my body
is once again resting new-year-naked, and i'll sigh a little,
and you'll be like *look hollie, it was you who ate that grape*

**don juan: a retranslation**

*on the myth that men who have had lots of different lovers will be better lovers, and for benny from accounts*

don juan, the most famous 'ladies' man' of literature
forwards the myth that men who shag a lot of different women
are much better lovers than benny from accounts, but

as some of you may know from experience, statistically,
heterosexual one-night stands are the sexual encounters
with the lowest likelihood of orgasm for women

so, in fact, benny from accounts,
who dated sally for two years
and then fiona for another seven months

is much more likely a better lover than
don juan, depending of course
on the communication in benny's relationships

also, don juan sounds really sexy in spanish
but juan just means john in english
and don, well,

it either refers
to a gentleman figure
or the leader of an organised-crime family

so though don juan has become
synonymous through books and plays
written by guys who also think

this supposed great seducer
was an expert lover
because he slept with loads of different women

the name don juan actually translates
more closely in modern english to
*john the shagger*,

who is statistically likely to be one of the
least able lovers, and definitely shitter
than benny from accounts

whose name in spanish
would be *señor benicio el contador*
which sounds sexy as fuck

**waterslide**

well, that's just great then, everything we learnt turned to tulips –
do you know how many magazines were folded,
so neat inside my needy teenage brain
when i could have been licking honey from the cold curve
of a pudding spoon? you call it honey, as if inside me
a hive buzzes sweetness to steal with a tongue tip
lord, all those articles i scoured, searching help growing up
*how to bag a man what to wear in summer how to fuck whilst*
*holding in your stomach how to wrap a single sexy lock of*
*hair around your index finger smiling gratefully as if your*
*candyfloss brain may be guzzled by a single, soggy raindrop*

we gathered top ten tips like saving seeds from extinction –
all that lingerie i persisted with, clingy, cheap fabric
sweating into metal poppers clipped into my crotch
scratching as if my vulva were an etch a sketch
the unbuttoning too fiddly for public toilets, nearly pissed myself
underwiring uplift slicing bloody crescent moons
at each side of my breasts, high heels scraping half the skin
from flimsy ankles as we strip-danced drunk in every club
for guys who pick their noses when they drive

now, on your sofa, me in my yellow striped pyjamas
filling in this online tax application, and you are stalagmite-excited
by the combination of keyboard taps and cotton
as you feed me another chip dipped in mayonnaise and mustard,
my left-hand typing formula into a multi-coloured spreadsheet,
right hand on your throbbing, as if i didn't even need to wash
all of those cars in that tiny, red bikini, all that swimwear
i couldn't even swim in, descending waterslides in panic
desperately clutching my fanny lips inside the minimal material

so i didn't flash the children – all those stupid fucking swimsuits,
all those stupid fucking tan lines, criss-cross hopscotch on my back,
shoulders burnt on purpose, holding in my stomach, inhaling,
in swimming pools and bedrooms,

they promised that's what sexy was, formula set in stone
in every tacky teenage bible – so what's this? your fingers
playing with the soft folds of a belly i was told would make boys vomit
as you ask me again about the spreadsheet i have built to calculate
income and expenses, my formulas revealed with a magic double click,
as if you prefer it when i'm comfortable, as if you prefer it
when i speak, as if you are not even bothered by all those
single strands of hair i've been curling round my fingers all these years,
as if you do not give a fuck what swimsuit i am wearing,
so long as i can race you down the waterslide, arms high up in the air

**house plants die if overwatered**

!                          !
   !
not me though!   flood my soil!   !
! let my leaf-flesh glug every hug and every cuddle!     drench me!
   !! until my roots are wearing wellies !!   !
water my worries!  ! with all the kisses!!  and caresses !!   !        !
!!   until the fountains in ancient town squares   !        !
over-spill from chubby cherubs' pissing willies!!!!!  !!! !!
!!!! let the marbled goddess breasts spill milk so abundantly  !
that!children!may!dive!beneath!the!surface!of!her!waters! !!   !
searching gold and copper coins! thrown in by tourists! making wishes!  !!!!
!!!! keep pouring!  !! !  !!!    and keep pouring!  !!!!!!!
!!till!!my!!sopping!!!skin!!!!glistens!!!beneath!!!this!!waterfall!of!!!want!!
!!!!!!   ! !!!!!!!      !!!!!!!!!!!!!!!!!!!!!!!!  !!!      !!!!!
leaves!         back!   raindrops!     an!          tap!      troupe!
     bouncing!       fat!          like!    iridescent!    dance!          !
                                      !           !
then leave me here,          !   !! l
                exhausted!       !
                  ! in this direct and scorching sun

## heirloom

*for gran, who kept telling me to take the jewellery i'd never seen her wear*

it's not your jewellery that i want gran,
it's your butter dish

so each time i go to slather a thick white slice of toast
with a thick bright slice of yellow

we'll be back in your reclining chairs
supper feast laid out

as you fast-forward through
the 'talking bits' of countdown

**croissants, warm**

love me soon, as much as the first day we met, but more
is that too much to ask?   i don't know

they say paintings fade in the sun
but there are friends i have known
since our legs swung too high for the floor
whose faces bring me even more joy than they did
when our mums still made dinner

how much fuller hugs feel
the more memories they hold

each year, blackberries sweeter
after waiting all winter and spring

my grandad told the same joke each time i saw him,
never got to the end for laughing too much

        i hope it is like this with you,

that my stories, once you hear them now over and over,
are like watching the same film each christmas

that my skin, which can never again be new to your touch
feels like stroking a favourite silk ribbon
stuffed in your pocket when days need a gift,
like delving back into favourite books,
finding constant new dreams in lines you forgot

let my body, now fully attuned to your touch
be like noticing snow start to fall

and still rushing to put on your hat and your gloves

like the ice-cream van announcing summer each year
with the same sudden joy

  let this love be like breakfast
            on weekends

no matter how many times i am lucky enough
to wake in the mornings,
  the sight of sunlight on skin
will never not fill me with a desperate desire
to fling off the sheets, rush down to the streets
    before the croissants sell out

**unforgettable**

from then on, church
became a passing glance

instead, we praised in records;
grandad insisting on silence from

us all. the record player resting in the
*other room*, we rarely went into, except

for nat king cole. lowered onto the turntable,
tender as a newborn, placed, finally asleep, into

its cot, and then we waited, as the needle dropped
and the air declared once more *let there be love*

# CHAPTER FOUR

## *Making Laws: Wolves and Warnings*

*Virginity is the ideal*
*of those who want to deflower*

– KARL KRAUS and JONATHAN MCVITY

Cela n'a pas duré plus que cinq minutes mais j'eus l'impression de passer une journée entière les jambes écartées nues sur cette table d'examen médical . . . Présumée coupable du crime le plus ridicule qui soit: celui d'avoir couché sans être mariée.

*It lasted no longer than five minutes but felt like I'd spent an entire day with my legs parted bare on this medical examination table . . . presumed guilty of the most ridiculous crime there is: sleeping with someone without being married*

– RIM BATTAL, *Je me regarderai dans les yeux*

I truly believe, maybe have to believe, that most people are kind; that most people want to protect children and teenagers and earn enough to take family or friends or a lover to see a movie once in a while.

Then the news headlines come calling, or you overhear conversations in bars, or see people on the street collecting money for anti-child-trafficking charities, or have your body grabbed by a stranger trying to climb into your car, and it all crumbles.

These are poems written whilst I felt that crumbling, veins fizzing in repulsion with the horrors of the human race – when I feel that, I write poems. And no, poetry does not get rid of any of this stuff, but it allows me not to let too much hate in; to turn grief and rage and bewilderment and terror and bleakness into something that helps me breathe again, get up, carry on and hopefully do something more practical; because merely feeling disgusted by shit never helped me do anything useful for anyone, myself included.

I initially opened this section with a quote from James Savile, a wealthy white English man who spent years abusing and raping children and teenagers and whose name on Wikipedia as of 2025 is still Sir James Wilson Vincent Savile OBE KCSG.

I watched an interview with him once, in which he expressed very frankly how he preferred girls to women, because girls know less. It offered me an understanding I didn't want into this sort of violence. When I think of this man, I most often think of the quote credited, perhaps falsely, to Mark Twain: *I've never wished a man dead, but I have read some obituaries with great pleasure.*

I would love to think that James Savile was a lone wolf roaming forests otherwise full of friendly faces, rather than part of a society still permeated with this predatory, paedophilic power.

If there is any argument for giving children and teenagers all the knowledge and confidence we possibly can, for me, it is that interview. Girls don't know enough. Women know 'too much'.

I think of what this person said each time I get asked to donate to anti-child-trafficking or anti-sex-trafficking charities; each time I hear supposed banter from men about going abroad to countries where it's OK because it's *legal over there*; every time I hear the 'I thought she was older' line; each time I read about young boys and girls dying by suicide after being bribed to send nudes, then money; every time I hear Andrew Tate followers telling young boys not to date girls over the age of nineteen, or tradwives telling the world how much they hate feminism, whilst staying home to care for a husband they can now legally leave if needed, who can no longer legally rape them in most countries in the world. I think about it when I recall being told that I'd struggle to find a boyfriend at school because I was getting good grades, and so I pretended for many years to understand less than I did, to giggle at things I didn't find funny, perfecting a kind of inane childish voice when talking to grown men lest I be told I'd lost my sense of humour, until my own daughter, aged eight, asked me one day why I was speaking *like a weird baby*. She was right, I was.

Whilst writing these poems I went for a doctor's appointment. The doctor was a woman. The appointment was to check for thrush. One of the first questions she asked me was whether I was in a relationship. Thrush is not an STI but fine, perhaps it was about protecting my partner and it can be passed on via contact.

She then asked if I was married. Annoyingly, instead of questioning why that would make thrush any more or less likely, or help in any way with the diagnosis, I just said 'no, I'm not'. She then asked me if it was a long-term relationship and on answering yes, she then said 'OK, we won't do an STI check then' and smiled, as if she were complimenting me on some sort of non-slut competition win. I didn't realise that wedding rings protected you like that, I thought it was just condoms. I thought of all the married people I knew and how many of them could easily have had an STI now unchecked by this doctor.

None of this is new of course, not the shaming, not the desperate need to teach kids about their rights and their bodies, not the existence of people who travel to countries so they can prey on less protected teenagers, not the use of shame to instil silence from victims, not the rich and powerful getting away with atrocities. As I write this, there are governments once again trying to lower the legal age of consent for both sex and marriage to nine years old. There are governments allowing ten-year-old rape victims to die in childbirth. And other governments suggesting introducing extreme chemical castration for convicted paedophiles and rapists.

I often fantasise about what would happen if the legal ages worldwide for marrying and for joining armies were raised to twenty-five years old. According to most recent studies, that's the age our brains are fully matured. I'd love for no more young people to be forced or pressured into marriage (and therefore often legal marital rape); for no more children or teenagers to be used as cannon fodder by distant grown-up commands. That would be nice.

In the meantime, here are some poems inspired by all the laws, and all the horror, and all the hate, and hope. It's probably not the section to read if you're looking for a pick-me-up.

There is so much to hate, so much to be angry about, so much to cry over, and if I don't turn it into something else, don't learn something from it, it will just sit inside me like coffin-rot, eating into my belief – and I do still believe it – that most people are lovely; that most people want love, just love, not power.

**grown woman speaking like a baby alert**

*for anyone, like me, who hasn't quite managed to shake this habit*

i'm not sure when it started; this affliction
me, a grown-ass woman, talking as if i still shat my nappy
simpering coyly, murmuring innocent responses to adult men
in the voice of a constipated sparrow    waitressing the world
love-me-love-me-lollipop stuck permanently in my mouth
head bowed to the ground as if my eyelashes were too heavy
for my fragile bashful face *oh don't ask me!! i know nothing!!!*

it wasn't when i was an actual baby, because then
i couldn't speak at all, because then
i was allowed to scream when i was hurting,
did not pretend to laugh when the tickling irritated
learnt to walk with such self-admiration
without worrying how unattractive it might make me
to other little babies; admired my learning body

yet here i am, thirty years on – ask me a question
and i will giggle automaton for no real reason
each opinion wrapped in fraying pastel ribbons
vomiting up sorrys as if my sentences
have a constant bout of salmonella;
exclamation marks queuing frantically in my emails
to decorate each statement with bunting and balloons
*oh my god, i am so sorry i am so sorry!!!!!!!!!!!!!!!!!!!!!*

~~forgive me!!!!~~ i am trying to delete them~~!!!!!!!~~
so much effort to unlearn everything
about growing up in pretty dresses –
do you remember that night, watching tele,

he said he didn't see the point of women over thirty.
he said it, then left to grab a biscuit,
as if nobody had died; words tossed onto the sofa
like a simple observation. like a favour. like a suicide letter.

## legal

*she said she was sixteen*, you say
and i realise you're one of them;
whose morals cling so devotedly
to laws you do not want to break –
don't mind if you break her

you google different countries
where teenagers are less protected
or else wait till sixteenth birthdays
as if candles on a cake make everything ok –
as if we should all applaud your patience

**this is how much faith we have**

of course we do not think it's all men
fuck, if we did, do you imagine we'd be here now
opening our doors to the plumbers or the taxi cabs
hugging our fathers and our uncles
letting kids play in the parks
attending classes with male students and male teachers
inviting boy friends round for dinner
dating strangers, getting married or divorcing,
giving birth to baby boys we sing to sleep each night
with lungs full of lullabies – if we actually thought,
yep, every single man, do you think we'd be so stupid
to live amongst them in clothing made of cotton,
bother nursing them in sickness, donating kidneys
in such unequal numbers, attend protests for their protection,
visit gravestones every month to place fresh flowers
cut at angles to absorb the water best,
walk down streets clutching only tiny keys for safety
in the hope, that despite the news we all hear
every single day, that *this* man will probably be great

**dear father, yes, today they voted in a _______**

that country we keep comparing to our own
despite the ocean in between. i know, i know, the same language
and all that, but dear father, today our government
sent a congratulating letter to the man who brags about
grabbing girls anytime he wants, yeah, i know
you have to be polite in politics, apparently,
so many leaders with giggling fingers held on triggers
salivating over power – bam! shake hands and smile for the camera –
a decision between genocide and rape, apparently,
a decision between healthcare and dying, school shootings
and national pride – has it always been this way, dad?
you've seen so much suffering in your life
and yet you carry on believing that most people
are kind, and most people are good,
and i agree, i think, but right now, it is difficult.
please tell me how you do it, when everywhere you look,
it's all bullets and bloodshed and abuse?

**imaginary father–son talk,**
**bored of my constant non-imaginary mother–daughter talks**

Pete passes Ben his jacket. *Remember not to rape anyone, my love, ok?*

*Oh my days dad, I know! You literally tell me that every time I step out the door.*

*Even if—* Pete starts again.

*I know, I know!*

Ben puts on his jacket. He knows the speech off by heart. *Even if I get horny or get an erection and I really want to have sex and I really like the girl and I can see her legs and her nipples through her top and I feel like I deserve it because I think she's been flirting with me and she turns me down or she's drunk, I get it! Seriously dad, stop worrying so much, I'm not going to rape anyone!*

Pete stands in the doorway and looks at his beautiful son, wishing the world were different. He begins to zip up Ben's jacket, which always annoys Ben, being treated like a baby when he is nearly sixteen. It is too warm to have his jacket zipped up anyway.

*I know, Ben, you've just got to be really careful. Especially when there's alcohol around.*

Ben rolls his eyes and breathes in.

*What's my number?*

*Dad!*

*Ben, what is my number? You need to know it off by heart in case you lose your phone and need me.*

*I know it.*

Ben recites the number.

*Good. And you call anytime ok. And if any of your friends seem like they might be getting aggressive with any of the girls, you just call me, ok, and I'll come.*

*Yes. Ok.*

*Promise me, Ben. If you think any of them might try to rape someone, do not let them wander off on their own, stick together and call me.*

*Yes, I promise, now can I please just go out? Dad, you always make me nervous before I go out. Not every boy rapes someone at a party you know?*

*Just be on your guard, ok. And stay away from the drink. It's not safe for boys to be drunk and I know there'll be alcohol there. Be careful is all I'm saying. Sorry Ben, I wish it wasn't like this.*

Ben takes his trainers from the shoe rack and starts to push his feet into them. He can feel his dad exhaling, ready. He knew there was no chance.

*You're not going out in those?*

Here we go. Ben stands up.

*Yes, dad, obviously, I'm literally putting them on. Please, I'll be fine. My shoes won't turn me into a rapist dad, Jesus Christ!*

*No, sorry son, you're not going out in them.*

*Dad! Everyone is wearing these! It's literally fashion, it doesn't mean anything.*

*Well, everyone isn't you and I don't want my son wearing shoes that he can so easily chase someone in. You either wear your non-rape shoes or you're not going to the party.*

*Are you serious dad? Literally no one wears those.*

*Look Ben. If you start to follow some poor girl and she's in heels, you need slower shoes otherwise she has no chance. I don't ask much of you but you're not going in those, it isn't safe and I'm only . . .*

*I know, I know! You're only doing it because you care.*

Ben pulls off his trainers and throws them down into the rack, takes the other pair of shoes. He puts them on, feeling the weight on his ankles immediately.

*Dad, I can hardly walk in them. They're so heavy.*

*It's your choice, Ben.*

*Fine*. Ben steps out the door, heaving one foot after the next.

*Remember, home by midnight.*

*Yes, dad.*

*I'm serious Ben, if you're going to be late, call us, otherwise we'll assume you've raped someone.*

*Oh my god, fine. Can I go now?*

*Yes. Be careful and call me for anything at all! Anything, remember!*

*Yes dad.*

*And have a lovely night, ok? Enjoy yourself my love!*

**when you think things might be getting better but then the french government try to ban a young athlete competing wearing a hijab but neither the netherlands olympic committee nor the international olympic committee ban a convicted child rapist from competing and you see the comments sections on news sites full of justifications for his violence saying that the twelve-year-old girl wanted to have sex and that the hijab is a sign of female oppression**

that's it. that's the poem.

## grown man; searching for virgin

he searches for 'virgin'
like browsing the library
for a book of blank pages
don't pretend you can't see
the appeal – only his story
to ink on their skin,
the bliss of no one before him
potentially better, secrets
kept secret, his word
both expert and master
seesaw            balanced
between bully and bird
how tempting, this one-sworded
duel to the death
the bible read only in latin
to poor congregations
forced illiterate, desperate
for something to trust
god gives a speech
to a crowd of gagged angels
the king, smiling, asks
your opinion, his gun
pressed direct to your head.
love, a command scratched
into your heart as you sleep

## riddle

if there are four times
as many teenage mothers
as teenage fathers

**just trust me on this**

beware
of the older guys
outside the gates, girls
the cute ones
with cars
you can't yet drive
glancing through the bars
like chastised puppies,
or else pouting
near the playground
once the school bell
has rung;
he nods as you pass him
i know, i *know*
his lips, lord,
hummingbird lashes
flicker
like finally
someone has noticed
how mature you really are;
aura of aftershave
only sold
behind counters
looks over
shy-bites his lips
as if he's
licking all the boredom
from your brain
and in your blood
that thrill
of being bulls-eye

heart bashing
like hollywood headboards
in run-down motels
after shootings
where a runaway girlfriend
if not dead already
screams out in pleasure
older badboy inside her
with a traumatic tale
all tears and no condom
but he's different,
this one,
and he wants you
and you want to be wanted
fuck love, who doesn't?
desire is a bandage
and glass stops
being see-through
when smashed
and he's actually shy
and he just thinks
you're really pretty
and believe me he is right,
you are incredible –

but he is not.
he is a grown-up
outside a college
with no kid
to pick up

enjoy the compliment,
and run.

masturbate about him
if you must

**saying no, when you're *nice and polite***

sometimes it feels like vomiting rocks
your stomach, rubble of crushed gravestones
jaws stuck shut with the weight of the word
backlogging in the back of your throat

as a toddler, you tantrumed it joyfully
orchestral screams in shops and on streets,
anchor-body flung to the floor like toppling tins
unashamed of eyes passing        until scolded,

you learn that politeness is quiet. is calm.
is respect for your elders. is plates on the table.
is smiling to customers. is curtsey to crowns.
ask why. *because i said so*

no

no

sometimes it feels too much for one person
searching a choir to hum it behind you
until the spotlight stops burning

keep trying. i promise it gets easier
say it. say it again,
until the toddler returns

## practice page

no no no no no no no no no no no no no no no no no no no no no no no no no
no no no no no no no no no no no no no no no no no no no no no no no no no
no no no no no no no no no no no no no no no no no no no no no no no no no
no no no no no no no no no no no no no no no no no no no no no no no no no
no no no no no no no no no no no no no no no no no no no no no no no no no
no no no no no no no no no no no no no no no no no no no no no no no no no
no no no no no no no no no no no no no no no no no no no no no no no no no
no no no no no no no no no no no no no no no no no no no no no no no no no
no no no no no no no no no no no no no no no no no no no no no no no no no
no no no no no no no no no no no no no no no no no no no no no no no no no
no no no no no no no no no no no no no no no no no no no no no no no no no
no no no no no no no no no no no no no no no no no no no no no no no no no
no no no no no no no no no no no no no no no no no no no no no no no no no
no no no no no no no no no no no no no no no no no no no no no no no no no
no no no no no no no no no no no no no no no no no no no no no no no no no
no no no no no no no no no no no no no no no no no no no no no no no no no
no no no no no no no no no no no no no no no no no no no no no no no no no
no no no no no no no no no no no no no no no no no no no no no no no no no
no no no no no no no no no no no no no no no no no no no no no no no no no
no no no no no no no no no no no no no no no no no no no no no no no no no
no no no no no no no no no no no no no no no no no no no no no no no no no
no no no no no no no no no no no no no no no no no no no no no no no no no
no no no no no no no no no no no no no no no no no no no no no no no no no
no no no no no no no no no no no no no no no no no no no no no no no no no
no no no no no no no no no no no no no no no no no no no no no no no no no
no no no no no no no no no no no no no no no no no no no no no no no no no
no no no no no no no no no no no no no no no no no no no no no no no no no
no no no no no no no no no no no no no no no no no no no no no no no no no
no no no no no no no no no no no no no no no no no no no no no no no no no
no no no no no no no no no no no no no no no no no no no no no no no no no
no no no no no no no no no no no no no no no no no no no no no no no no no

## blood, in the world of wolves

*in the hope we will stop telling girls*
*'you're a woman now', when their period begins*

*can you name a country where boys*
*are legally allowed to marry adult women?*

– CHLOE LAWS

when the blood began, they told her
she was *woman* now; *woman, woman*
word heavy as a coffin, childhood done
and dusted; snap the chicken bone, girl,
throw it to the foxes; it is over

and as she bled, she heard *woman,*
*woman, woman* as she wept,
believing this the end,
body shapeshifted from childhood
with the first egg released

what now, then? must she accept
the grown wolves glancing at her body,
shadows of paws and pounces
slowly sniffing at her skin, wedding dresses
sewn in sizes far too small to be holy –

*but she is ready to bear children now!*
they grunt, wolves in courtrooms
once again, nodding, declaring, saliva dripping
from lips, bloody for another kill, legislation,
menstruation declared evidence of womanhood

oh stupid gods of science, where are you?
protect them! tell them! spit it in their fucking faces!
the blood is the *beginning* of transition,
will not protect her childish bones from breaking
with the weight of womb; she is not ready

to be anybody's mother, your bloody wife;
little girl, do not listen to the lies
the fairytales were written as a warning of wolves –
do not let them convince you the moon is full
when the moon is still waning,

i am so sorry the forests are still swarming
bleed well; you are no *woman* yet
do you hear me? you have years left
to be a child, little girl, good god,
you should have years left to be a child

## stubble, in the world of war

*in the hope we will stop leaving boys' deaths*
*out of war loss statistics, once they reach adolescence*

*For his teeth seem for laughing round an apple.*
*There lurk no claws behind his fingers supple;*
*And God will grow no talons at his heels,*
*Nor antlers through the thickness of his curls.*

– WILFRED OWEN, 'Arms and the Boy'

when the stubble came, they told him
he was *man* now; *man*,
word heavy as a cannon, childhood done
and dusted; snap the chicken bone, boy,
throw it to the foxes; it is over

and as he stood crying with his mother
rubble buried beneath fingernails
searching and screaming and searching
the headlines repeated *women and children*
    *women and children*

what age must a young boy become
before he's erased as a victim? thirteen?
sixteen? no longer shielded by childhood
hierarchies of innocence and sympathy
spitting him out when stubble shows;

shouldn't we stop separating the sadness?
it is all devastation; women and children
murdered amongst brothers and fathers,
grandfathers, lovers, and friends

boys holding hands in the playgrounds
bleating hearts equally hopeful for futures
before the blossom is bombed; grow well son,
you have years left to be a child, do you hear me?
good god, you should have years left to be a child

**man-hater**

most men are killed by men
most blood of men is spilled by men
most men are raped, groomed
abandoned, tortured and abused by men
most men are drugged by men
most men must fight because of men
most men walk home more hurriedly
at night because of other men
most men are shot by men
most men are gassed by men
most men are forced in gangs,
are given guns, are sent to war by men
most men are stabbed by men
most men are bribed and robbed by men
most men fear for the life
of boys they love because of men

**romantic, apparently**

black and white photograph
beautiful boys we call soldiers
barely legal, lean out
of government train windows,
blow kisses towards the lips
of future widows

**most people**

once a month at least, most people hold a saucepan
in their hands, stir soup, make extra just in case

on mondays, most people wake up hoping children
will be safe, notice roses on a roadside and sigh

most people make love nervously, worry afterwards
whether their breath was fresh enough

get embarrassed buying underwear, apologise
when crying, blush when offering their seat to a stranger

on the hour every hour, most people are not newsworthy,
every day we are watching the extremes

most people do not make headlines,
hands full of weapons. most people are searching

through the rubble, hoping loved ones may laugh
with loved ones once again. drawing curtains, searching

for just a little rain that roots may glug enough to blossom
into fruit again. there's too much sorrow, this is certain

but most people bring a cup of warmth to loved ones
in the morning, pray for peace when they are praying

# CHAPTER FIVE

## *Making Love*

*Where the myth fails, human love begins.*

– ANAÏS NIN

*Love doesn't just sit there, like a stone,*
*it has to be made, like bread;*
*remade all the time, made new*

– URSULA K. LE GUIN

This section is called 'Making Love'. I have hated this phrase most of my life and I am determined not to hate it any more. I first heard the phrase as a teenager and I was like 'urgh, gross, who says that?!' Then 50 Cent clinched the deal in his album *Get Rich or Die Tryin'*. I was obsessed with this album and in one of the songs he explains that he's into sex but not into making love. I was like, *yeah, yeah me either Fifty, making love is for losers.*

I found the phrase 'making love' so terrible, such a cringy way to describe having sex. I was much more comfortable with the idea of violence than 'love-making'; had seen a lot more movie scenes of fights or really quick bent over intercourse or even sexual assault than extended loving intimacy, which is a bit shit really, but probably fairly common. (*Dirty Dancing* was the one standout antidote to this, which I watched about one hundred and twenty times.)

At the age of thirty-five, I stumbled across Ursula Le Guin's quote, repeated at the start of this section, comparing making love to making bread, and instead of thinking of the phrase in some creepy voiceover, I considered it practically for the first time in my life.

Making love.

Making . . . love.

Making. Love.

Making.

Love.

It was like making anything. Making friends. Making time for people. Making somebody smile. Making peace with yourself. Making soup. And I thought, actually, I do make love, I make it all the time and I want to make more of it and I don't want to hate the phrase any more.

I love the idea that love has to be something you make. Like you can literally put it together; make it however you want, with whatever fabrics or materials or words or ingredients or body parts suit you best.

The more I repeat this phrase with a little more space between the two words (in a non-slimy voice), the cooler I think it sounds. Like a jigsaw I'm putting together. Like a recipe I'm learning to cook better so that I can invite friends round to eat. Yes, I want to make . . . love. Of course I fucking do. What's the other option? Making nothing? Making hate? I am sure I have made those things too, so even more reason for me to get on with making more . . . love.

As well as calling this section 'Making Love', I have called every single poem in the section 'making love', because that's what they're all about and because I figured if I write and say this phrase enough times, I will stop finding it disgusting or weird or disrespectful to 50 Cent and it will just become a normal way for me to think about relationships and sex and life in general.

Every time I write a poem I am making love. Every time I cook for someone. Every time I touch. Every time I send postcards. Every time I hug. Every time I say sorry when I am a prick. Every time I clean my house for my mum arriving even though she tells me I don't have to and that she doesn't care about that shit. Every time I stick the kettle on for a friend. And yes, every time I have sex.

I hope by the time I die I will have made as much love as I possibly can in the time and budget constraints of this life. I hope I will make enough love to have many, many people feel more love because of me.

And yes, I am still totally embarrassed to write this because I am outing myself as a lovestruck soppy mess, but I am. I can't be bothered holding back any more, playing it cool, trying to impress 50 Cent, pretending I'm a hater. If love isn't cool, then fuck it, neither am I. I love love and I want to make it as much as I can before I can't.

**making love**

cheapest room in the hotel
no windows on the wall
but the bath was hot and full, and you were in it

smiling, silhouetted
lips already sweating
arms curving out a space where i should sit

and so i stripped, lay back against you
shadows steaming, saying nothing,
occasionally kissing as we hugged

*how strange it is* i thought
as we dried our gasping bodies
that this is not considered *making love*

**making love**

to her it was a brave new quest
a hopeful first
a wholesome snog

the scent of lynx
mingled with vanilla thrills –
her tongue, his tongue

to the teachers
it was two year ten
detentions

i guess this love
is all about perspective

**making love**

in the grand scheme of things, you've done nothing – virgin!
learn every european language, and at least two hundred others
saunter across the continent of africa alone
in conversations you will never comprehend –
visit one small village library, on one bookshelf
how many pages you will never turn, knowledge never known,
stories undiscovered beneath torchlit bedtime sheets –
that patch of park you pass every single day to work
how many flowers orchestra unnoticed?
what birdsong have you noted? which flavours
of ice cream does your tongue still long to memorise?
dip your timid toes into the ripples of fifty different lakes
and a myriad of other waterways still shimmer unswum –
most people who pass you by are strangers, always will be,
and your body, endless nerves of rolling ocean,
how many currents still tingle undiscovered inside your sapling skin?
write a list of all the songs you've never sung
and you will die with the pen still in your hand

you are seventy per cent water and ninety-nine per cent virgin
such virgins we all are

i had never seen the moon through a telescope
till last night, feet tiptoeing your bedsheets
to reach the open attic window like a child peaking a garden
overgrown with yellow roses, only ever knowing red
your binoculars held virgin-tight against my new stargazer eyes,
moon-virgin that i was, yellow-rose-virgin –
and now, still, i have never seen a zebra or an octopus,
never been to dundalk, never kissed
inside the glitter-green umbrella of a willow tree in rainfall,

i have never seen tomorrow's sunrise, or the next day's –
i have never fed a donkey, never double skimmed a pebble,
never slept inside a treehouse, never heard a parrot speak,
most of the melodies made by most of the world's violins
are virgin to my ears. i have only just discovered there are carrots
that are not orange, and despite my love for peaches, i have never
picked fresh peaches from a peach tree in a country
where peaches grow on peach trees, never plucked one
from its branches, never stuffed it in my open mouth
until all the peachy sweetness dribbles down my sticky virgin chin
fresh-peach-virgin that i am! purple-carrot-virgin! tomorrow's-sunset-virgin!

stroll down one busy city street, there is enough human chatter
to fill an infinity of joke books,

and we walk on, as if we're all big adults now,
as if there's nothing new to love

## making love

**Across**

3. a person creating something without a clear plan (from French)
7. pouring your heart and soul so passionately into something you are doing – loving, cooking, painting, writing – that a little piece of you remains within it (from Greek)
8. the conversation at the table that carries on going once the meal is over (from Spanish)
10. the anticipation of waiting for someone to arrive and so you keep running outside your house to check if they are here yet (from Inuit)
11. accidently eating all of the dinner, devouring the whole lot despite already being full, because the food is so flipping delicious (from Georgian)

**Down**

1. the urge to pinch or squeeze something that is unbearably cute (from Filipino)
2. the art of listening to each other and being able to gauge one another's mood (from Korean)
4. moonlight shining on water (from Turkish)
5. the time of day when it is becoming dark but not yet fully dark and the light is low and feels like it's somehow glowing (from English)
6. tenderly running your fingers through a loved one's hair (from Brazilian Portuguese)
9. to get up very early to hear the birdsong and feel the stillness of the world before all the bustle of the human day begins (from Swedish)

**gloaming gigil meraki sobremesa nunchi**

**cafuné gökotta iktsuarpok shemomedjamo gumusservi**

**bricoleur**

**Answers**

1. gigil 2. nunchi 3. bricoleur 4. gumusservi 5. gloaming 6. cafuné
7. meraki 8. sobremesa 9. gökotta 10. iktsuarpok 11. shemomedjamo

## making love

when two people speak arabic in front of me, i panic
the same way i panic when gymnasts, apparently wingless,
born of bone and muscle like my own, turn spirals mid-air,
or when my aunty bakes passion fruit pavlova, as if it's simple
to bake passion fruit pavlova; how can i call myself a lover
when i know nothing of the language in which my favourite words
are sung? some call it limitless, arabic, recount possibilities of poetry
that english cannot fathom, so many words for love, for loving
while i chase romance with a dictionary a quarter of the thickness,
unpacking summer picnics with no punnet of strawberries
– all the ways that i could love you, if only i spoke arabic –
i'm told that love songs in arabic are like cloud above cloud,
the endless thirst of flowers, drifting asleep inside a raindrop
awakening to a world magnified ten times more gorgeous
through the falling teardrop glass; and here i am,
breathing in a conversation on the bus, understanding nothing,
scrappling for scant treasures stolen into english
to hold upon my tongue like a jealous, rusting typewriter
at a desk with no view of the mountains: say elixir, *elixir*,
say alchemy, say algebra, say chemistry, say monsoon,
say apricot, say zenith, say zero, say satin, sash and saffron,
say lemon, lime and orange, say sherbet, syrup, sorbet –
arabic, what sweetness you have brought us, i panic when you speak,
knowing i will never comprehend even a handful of your beauty;
your words, a thousand butterflies hovering above me
like sequins in the great azul,
i hold my hand out, hopeful

## making love

*for gran, who often told me about her first boyfriend who, on finding out she lived in a council house, demanded her father repay him the fiver he'd spent on a handbag*

in the films, he flies her to paris   just for dinner
        champagne, caviar   flies back
                i do not need romance like that

as a girl, i daydreamed in casinos and black satin
diamonds were your best friend    belted in ballads
in the pop songs, if you love her  a handbag  designer

director shouts action
a rich man watches me descend a flight of stairs
clips sparkles around my collarbone

in the bedroom
scream loudly
when he cums

last night, i asked my brain to empty,
to empty and begin again
those scenes, they were never my own writing

love, what do you dream of once you have unlearnt every script?

strip the bed of all that spotless white cotton,
cocaine, choking,
pool parties, private islands

these are not my fantasies, they never were
postcards from the usa  hollywood  millionaires

placed there by projectors

in reality,

i feel sexiest in silence
crave touch like feathers falling
lust, a raindrop hitting metal

cocaine tastes like shit, and i couldn't give a fuck
about a necklace made from mining

so hold my hand below the sky
the sky, hung just above our heads
announcing dawn and dusk every day in neon,
then stars, stars, endless campfires of the night
you can see them from anywhere
so long as you look up

so paris if you want, if you can

otherwise, just let me nap against your heartbeat
tiptoe secrets with your lips along my spine
your tongue inside my thighs like sealing a love letter

give me your fears and an hour with your hands
give me orgasms and stories from your childhood
kindness and time,

naked, let me see you,
all those candles, all those flames

**making love**

*before all the noise begins again*
slow dance with me please
because i do not want to talk
and i do not want to think
about tomorrow or the world

for just three dancing minutes
press your heartbeat to the heartbeat
in my chest, as if we've only just
been born and know nothing
except music and warm milk

for two more minutes, dance
it doesn't matter if you *can't*
we do not even need to move
your arms around my waist will do
just hold me,

for the final sixty seconds of this song
your skin is hope against my skin,
and i might be wrong, but i wonder
if this is everything,

so hold me for the final twenty
hold me for the final ten

**making love**

to her it was a hushed escape
a shield of stone
a loop of salt

door safely locked
for sacred touch
as music surged then sunk

to the bouncers
an illicit shag
in the toilet of a nightclub

i guess this love
is all about perspective

# making love

| u | o | y | o | u |  |  | y | o | i | l | e | t | i | l | n | e | h | w |
|---|---|---|---|---|---|---|---|---|---|---|---|---|---|---|---|---|---|---|
| o | y |  | u |  | l | d |  | t | o | i |  | t | o | i | t | h | w | s |
| h | e | n | e | h | e |  | u |  | c |  | c |  | t | o | e | w | s | t |
| w | h | e | l | h | e |  | p | c | i | l | i | c |  | t | l | i | t | e |
| h |  | n | d | t | h | e |  | b | u | b | l | i | c |  | t | o | e | l |
|  | r | u |  |  | t | h | e |  | p | u | b | l | i | c |  | t | l | i |
| h | u | o | y | n |  | t | h | e |  | p | u | b | l | i | c |  | t | o |
|  | r | u | o | i | t | h | e |  | p | l | b | l | i | c |  | t | o | i |
| h |  | r | u |  | i | n | l | b | u |  | c | i | c |  | t | o | i | l |
| d | h |  | r | r |  | i | n |  | t | t | o | t |  | t | o | i | t | e |
| n | d | h |  | e | r |  | i | n |  | t | h | o | i | o | i | l | s | t |
| u | n | a | h | y | e | i | n |  | t | h | e |  | p | i | l | e | t | s |
|  | d | n | a | r | y | e | r |  | i | n |  | p | u | l | e | t | s | w |
| u |  | d | r | d | e | r |  | i | n |  | p | u | t | e | t | s | w | h |
| n | r |  | d |  | r | e | r | n | i | n |  | t | h | e | s | w | h | e |
| d | e | r | h | e | r | y | e | r |  | i | n | h | e |  | p | u | b | n |
| e | r |  | t | h | d | r | y | e | r |  | i | n | h | p |  | p | u | b |
| r |  | c | h | e |  | d | r | y | e | r | n |  | t | h | e |  | p | u |

**making love**

remind me of your body now and then
beneath the table, let legs overlap a little
remind me how warm skin is in winter

in the bed, snuggle in
link your fingers like a seatbelt round my belly
warm blood water bottle behind my back

take my hand
walking down the frosted street
remind me i am living

**making love**

walking wordless
but between us
those lucky brushing hands
find each other
as they always seem to do
when there is nothing more to say
i have stories, but you've heard them
or you haven't, either way
my lips are tired, and the news
is too horrific to discuss
in this dimming light
but our hands,
clasped to one another
like roots below the forest floor
in silence, sharing water

in silence, sharing water
roots below the forest floor
spread hope to one another
like human hands
clasped between heartbeats
in the dimming light
the trees are standing stoic
as if solitary creatures
but beneath them
nutrients and warnings
gifted one another
like a mother's sudden clutch
at the clifftop of a frantic road
or two contented lovers
walking, wordless

**making love**

i just want to fuck, and when i say fuck i mean breathe, and when i say fuck i mean gaze at the stars for as long as my neck can hold up my skull to the sky, i mean swallowing night like a spoon filled with blackberry syrup, like fingers stained purple from fruit gobbled straight from the bushes, heaving with sweetness, plucked between thorns, i want to fuck like petals pouting for wasps, like potato mashed hot into butter and salt as the radio plays songs i forgot i know all the words to, i want to fuck like everyone knows all the words to songs they forgot, like no one you love has ever been bruised, like firefighters always save everyone burning, i want to fuck like moonlight spilt milk on the ocean, like lighthouse beams turn towards ships nearing shadowy rocks, i want to fuck like everyone knew how to swim, like there *were* enough lifeboats, like black forest gateau is easy to make, like sap oozing slow from the bark of the maple drizzled on pancakes flipped whole as your plate now drowns in the cold puddled gold glossing your glazed, guiltless lips while you stuff the whole stack in your cheeks, i want to fuck like a nap after eating, like a nap after fucking, like food in the bedroom, like stroking my hair while we're kissing, like touching in secret, like sunshine, like silence, by which i mean mountains, like climbing, like caverns, like fireflies, like falling, i want to fuck like i'm falling, like everyone's falling, like nobody knows how to land, like licking the edge of a rainbow and tasting the colours of hot splintered rain, like a raindrop burst open on parched earth below soon to be gratefully sucked up the stem of a wild garlic's green, greedy throat

**making love**

to her it was a forest den
midnight stars cooling flesh

unpeeling fabrics just enough
to taste each other's flavours best

to the police, an illegal act
in the bushes outside tesco

i guess this love
is all about perspective

## making love

*for michael, who loves spirals*

i ask for more kisses on my neck, so you give me more kisses on my neck. hard to say sometimes but skin cannot speak, relying on the tongue to spill its secrets. so i tell you i'd love more kisses on my backbone and my hips, so you give me more kisses on my backbone and my hips. hard to ask sometimes but skin cannot speak, relying on the tongue to spill its secrets, so

**making love**

*good morning*, and towards the dawn one million sunflowers slowly turn.
you yawn. feet still half-asleep upon the skin-warm sheets find mine.
in the garden, one by one, daisies unfurl petals for the light. pink-tipped,
white eyes open to the day. i turn my cheek towards your face. you grin,
pull me closer. in the ocean, a pufferfish paints patterns on the seabed,
shifting sands into ephemeral circles with its belly. i feel your chest
against my backbone, breathing. no one knows if it is the finer feel of sand
or the beauty of the mate's imagination that attracts a passing interest.
in the vase that was your mother's in the kitchen, red and yellow tulips
slowly twist green stalks towards the window. you sweep my hair aside.
distant sparrows start to sing. under my t-shirt, your fingers begin playing
with the softness of my stomach. in a sun spot, lions nuzzle, stretching limbs,
manes tickle noses. wild lilacs in a forest far away release sweet perfume
to a swarm of passing bees. the great male argus, over-dressed again,
struts past waiting suitors. giraffes lap fresh urine from potential lovers.
you sit up. hippos wallow belly up in mud. i pull your t-shirt up.
mating lemurs start to share each other's scent. newly naked skin
stripes with sunflecks and shadows of the ever-shifting weather.
you duck under the covers. fruit bats, clung upside down to branches,
begin intensive cunnilingus. snakes weave shapes into one another.
in the sky, swifts mate mid-flight. kangaroos bounce back to back.
bonobos begin to masturbate profusely in giant orgies to ward off war.
i put my hair into a ponytail. outside the window, a sudden gust of breeze
sweeps up a thousand dandelion seeds to flirt across a field of waiting soil
where butterflies hover in their hundreds over lavender and hollyhocks
and a hummingbird, now pollen-drenched, bathes in the pale red clutch of petals.
your breathing is my breathing. is slowing. the sun is fully risen. after mating,
dolphins jump amongst the waves. you lay a blushing cheek upon my chest
as if my heartbeat were a long-forgotten song playing underwater. in the desert
a sudden rainfall allows four young frogs to dance outside again. we giggle,
doze for ten more minutes, faces to the sun. the otters won't stop cuddling.

**making love**

*softly, and for longer*
is all she ever really wanted to say
instead, she said nothing or *yes*,
she said, *good*, she said, *mmm*

there are books about pleasure on her book shelf
as if she had no idea what she loves
as if she hadn't known for years
as if her hands could not have told her time ago
everything written there in ink

sometimes back up is needed to believe your own body
how easy, alone, to keep going, *softly, and for longer*
her friend suggested therapy,
she doesn't need therapy, at least not for this

she just needed the truth to be easier
desire, a loudspeaker,
backing choir to be believed
for her skin to be a simple conversation

as if once upon a time, in a tale untouched
by serpents, sluts and virgin births
our own burning bodies were the plot

# making love

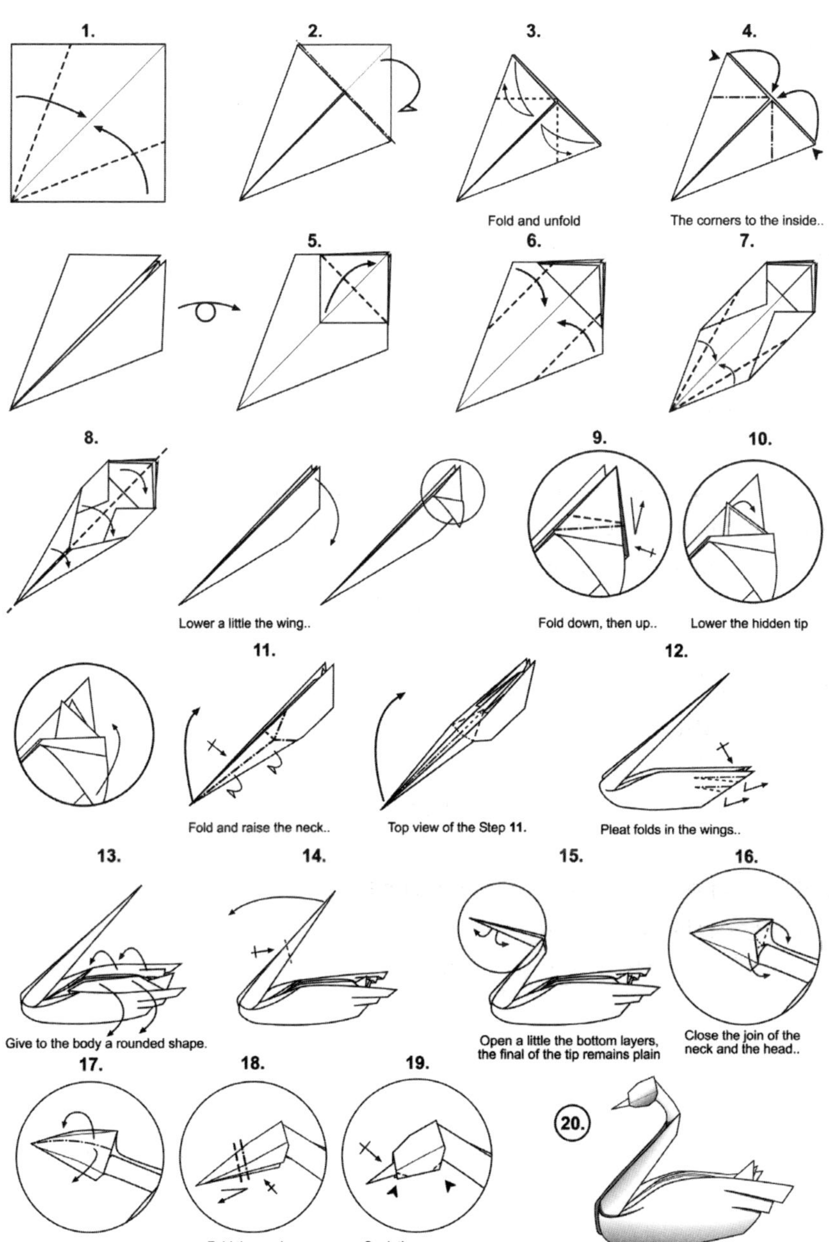
1.
2.
3.
4.
Fold and unfold
The corners to the inside..
5.
6.
7.
8.
9.
10.
Lower a little the wing..
Fold down, then up..
Lower the hidden tip
11.
12.
Fold and raise the neck..
Top view of the Step 11.
Pleat folds in the wings..
13.
14.
15.
16.
Give to the body a rounded shape.
Open a little the bottom layers, the final of the tip remains plain
Close the join of the neck and the head..
17.
18.
19.
20.
Fold the peak..
Sunk the corners..

**making love**

*for everyone who has taught me how to*

with this cup of soup, i love you
        with this surprise of honeyed toast in bed
        with these storybooks i read you
        with this kiss upon your forehead

with this towel warmed and hot tap run
        to fill a blessed bathtub full
        candles lit like sudden love
        wax the scent of ceasefire deals

with the stars i cannot steal, but still
        will take your hand to rush outside
        each time the night is clear enough
        to map the black of ancient lights

and when time between us beckons
        with these arms, i'll wave goodbye
        smiling from the doorway
        until the second you are gone

and with this door, forever open
        for your return

**making love**

as toddlers,
we splodged our hands
into trays full of paint

printed sheets of plain paper
with keen, messy palms

this is my body now
covered
in life, full of colour

all the touches
that turn me to art

## acknowledgments

### for the book

although there's only one name on the cover of this book
don't be fooled into believing one person did the work;
to such elegant editors, rhiannon then caitlin, for your chats
and your corrections, your encouragements, suggestions,
your stripping of the scrappy parts of drafts that came before;
how expertly you know when to hold me back from rambling –
how politely you say lovely things about the other chapters
before suggesting any cuts; to joelle, for your final sparks
and shimmering support; clara, for your endless back
and forths and forth and backs on everchanging email chains,
constantly delightful despite your likely lack of sleep;
to lilly for your colours and adept imagination; to nithya
and to lynn, for your patience and your expert hunter eyes
without which this book would still be steeped in my mistakes –
spelling errors, grammar lapses, words left out of sentences,
quotes misquoted or miscredited pointed out to me by family
or readers once the book's already printed; to the typesetters
and the designers, nico taylor, jack flag, who turned the pages
into portraits of each poem and made fine artwork of the
covers and fancy flaps; to laxmi for reminding me how sacred
mothers' outlines are; to becky, and rhiannon once again,
for making this all happen; to the legal team who stop me
getting sued or put in prison; to the libraries i can sit in
without spending any money, soaking up the stories;
to the bookshops and the booksellers who place me
kindly on their brimming shelves; to my cousins, tracy,
erin, lucy, who often shift the stock to put me at the front;
to the readers who pick me up and take me home
to flick through in their bedrooms, or on buses, or on beaches,

or else sit in darkened venues, listening; without all your
gorgeous help this collection would still be a shoebox full of poems,
scribbled, scrumpled paper stars beneath my bed.

**for the inspiration**

luckily, so much love in my life so far, i've no mind
where to start here – perhaps best with my mother.
when i was five, she let me eat my dinner in the bathtub;
two potato waffles and ketchup on a floating plastic plate,
and i sat in bubbled paradise, no-shits-given-naked,
scoffing hot potato, learning the meaning of true
and simple love; and for my skin, which will not stop
chorusing in water or when sun glosses its surface;
to my aunty viv, and poppy fields, and swear words,
swivels and scented candles, your incense ever-burning;
to aunty jan and aunty june for your constant caring,
to my grandmas, for forgiveness and tender conversations;
to gee for his defence of a stretching pregnant belly,
for his kind and joy-filled fathering; to my parents,
always loving, always laughing, who did not tell me
scary stories about sluts or shame or hell; to my superhero
'cousin' and her superhero parents; to my daughter,
who stopped me speaking like a baby to older men,
who stopped me letting my split ends get worse;
yes, i am a soppy mess, embarrassing and thankful
every second since you were born; to michael,
for so much love, wonder and encouragement,
for early nights, and elfin queens; your efferfizzing heart
is an endless thrill to share in; to simon,
for your laughter at the market and affordable
fresh vegetables, so i might live as long as possible,

which is my only selfish dream; my body is made
mostly of your onions and potatoes; for gemma,
in general, and for sharing audre lorde's writings
on protest and the erotic, making every day more candlelit;
to shirley and billy for your welcomes, warmth and fervour,
and to cory, who sold us her mother's home last year
and left me full of feelings and free furniture,
including a wobbly wooden desk which I think
is ensorcelled and makes me feel very poety,
and to all the writers and strangers who have taught me
and inspired me; to shelly-ann and julie, laura, rowena,
maddy, jo, kathryn, hanna, tammy, vim, helen, lj, kasia
and kamila, sandeep, sally, juliet, carly and fiona,
laurie, kat, gemma, musa, michael, caroline and jodie
and all the other grateful friendships that make daily life
a giggle and a hug; and to the dawn, splatted each morning
like a hot neon mess across the sky; and for sleep,
which i am grateful to get more of these days;
and for children, the most inspiring of all humans.

# CREDITS

P 5: https://www.instagram.com/p/C8KWnikKFP4/

P 24: Epigraphs from 'What you don't know about intimacy in World War I' by Alexander Meddings (2017), https://historycollection.com/dont-know-intimacy-world-war/

P 31: Epigraph from Maya Angelou, *Letter To My Daughter* (New York: Random House, 2009).

P 59: Epigraph from Ada Limón, 'Lover'. Reproduced by permission of Corsair, an imprint of Little, Brown Book Group, Carmelite House, 50 Victoria Embankment, London EC4Y 0DZ.

P 59: Epigraph from Audre Lorde, 'Learning from the 60s', address at Harvard University, February 1982.

P 65: Epigraph from Helene Hanff, *84, Charing Cross Road* (New York: Grossman Publishers, 1970).

P 87: Epigraph from Karl Kraus and Jonathan McVity, *Dicta and Contradicta* (Urbana: University of Illinois Press, 2001).

P 87: Epigraph from Rim Battal, *Je me regarderai dans les yeux* (Paris: Bayard Editions, 2025).

P 108: Epigraph from Chloe Laws, TEDxTeessideWomen talk, 'Misandry Myths', 2024.

P 115: Epigraph from Anaïs Nin, *Mirages: The Unexpurgated Diary of Anaïs Nin, 1939–1947* (Ohio: Swallow Press, 2013).

P 115 : Epigraph from Ursula K. Le Guin, *The Lathe of Heaven* (New York: Avon Books, 1971).

P 137: Shutterstock.

## INDEX OF POEMS